PULSE
to
PLANET

Celebrating
30 Years of Publishing
in India

Praise for *Pulse to Planet*

'*Pulse to Planet* is a thoroughly documented warning and a call to action: the world is in danger, and a comprehensive response is required to confront the threats it is facing. Our response will fall short if we do not understand the complex connections between humans, other species and their shared environment. An enlightened thinker and an elegant writer, Srinath Reddy discusses these connections in a gifted way and makes a compelling case in defence of future generations.'

Professor Julio Frenk
President, University of Miami
Former Dean, Harvard T.H. School of Public Health
Secretary of Health (Minister) of Mexico (2002–06)

'Srinath Reddy has distilled his lifelong pursuit of science, medicine and public health into a remarkable guide for young people on how to promote a healthy world. In under 300 pages, Reddy covers a remarkable range of topics, all the way from individual genes and behaviour to the global environment. Reddy's vast erudition shines on every page, in words that are crystal clear, humane and full of wisdom. Young people the world over will benefit enormously from this unique guide for healthy lives on a healthy planet.'

Professor Jeffrey Sachs
Director, Center for Sustainable Development,
Columbia University
President, UN Sustainable Development Solutions Network
Former Director, Earth Institute

'A philosopher of medicine and no less than a master of its intricacies, Srinath gives us in the distilled wisdom of this book a veritable Principia Medica of our times—for those who need, those who teach and those who practice that science. He enables us to look upon health and its care not as an arcane discipline but an aspect of life under changing environments and unforeseen challenges. Mastery of theme combines with that of the written word to give us a book that instructs, engages and delights.'

Gopalkrishna Gandhi
Former Governor, West Bengal
Former High Commissioner to South Africa and Sri Lanka

'*Pulse to Planet* is an extremely well-written and articulate book, which is easy to understand, and with a flow that makes it a compelling read. What excited me most was to see the connectedness and the awareness from a reader's perspective become very clear. Solutions, which are technology-enabled, and a willingness to share for global common good are to be encouraged by each and every one of us, howsoever small. Environmental degradation is real and affects the health of everyone and of our future generations. Overall, a great contribution by Dr K. Srinath Reddy, which I would recommend to any reader.'

S. Ramadorai
Chairman, Public Health Foundation of India
Former CEO and MD, Tata Consultancy Services

'This is a timely and eye-opening read that not only outlines the threats that face our planet and humanity but one that critically illustrates a clear path forward. Drawing on his eminent career as a physician and cardiologist, Reddy aptly draws on the key ingredients for both our individual and collective health and demonstrates how intricately linked these are to the precious ecosystems that we inhabit. An inspiring read for anyone who cares about the future of our planet and wants to shape the global society that we all live in for the better.'

Baron (Prof.) Peter Piot
Former Director, Handa Professor of Global Health,
London School of Hygiene & Tropical Medicine
Advisor to the President of the European Commission
Winner of WHO Lifetime Achievement Award for Global
Leadership (2023)

'This is a wonderful book with an inspiring vision for the future. It is beautifully written, explaining complex subjects in ways that can educate us all and help us understand how we depend on each other and the whole planet for our health and well-being. I thoroughly recommend it and will be sending copies to friends and family.'

Lord Nigel Crisp
Co-Chair, All-Party Parliamentary Group on Global Health,
United Kingdom
Former Chief Executive, National Health Service of England

'A passionate call for leadership by today's youth to combat planetary climate change, the existential threat of our times. Focusing on health as the best summative indicator of sustainable development, this book connects the health of people and our planet in a powerful analysis. The best way of avoiding "civilizational suicide" is the "admirable idealism" of the next generation, who are our best hope for sustainable health development.

'A tour de force, this analysis of how human and planetary health depends upon both internal balance (homeostasis) and connectivity (people-to-people and people-to-environment). Genes may be inherited but they are not fixed, influenced by how they are expressed—via epigenetics. Human genes are complemented by billions of bacteria that reside in our gut and skin. Nutrition is more than diets of individual nutrients, but also agricultural and food systems. Health determinants are shaped by not only individual behaviour but also systemic economic, educational and social forces, especially powerful commercial interests.

'These forces are generating a fresh pattern of diseases; "syndemics" like chronic diseases of obesity and new threats like COVID-19 and climate catastrophe. Steadily increasing longevity is no longer guaranteed. The old may have wisdom but lack the will and tools that can be mobilized by the young to overcome the power of business and politics.

'A mandatory book by a world-leading cardiologist (pulse) and a giant in global public health (planet), this book will energize the young, inform the medical professions and remind the old that the future belongs to the next generation!'

Dr Lincoln Chen
President Emeritus, China Medical Board
Former Chair, Department of Population and International
Health, Harvard School of Public Health

'I congratulate Professor Reddy on this book that gives primacy to health as an individual and societal good but makes it clear that such health is closely and inextricably linked to planetary health, which is achievable only through social solidarity and collective action. The range of evidence is impressive and the prose lucid and compelling. This book not only presents challenges but is clear about the solutions that must be embraced if the link between pulse and planet is to be preserved and strengthened. I recommend it highly.'

Sir George Alleyne
Chancellor, University of the West Indies
Director Emeritus, Pan American Health Organization
Former UN Secretary General's Special Envoy on HIV-AIDS

'As the world is facing an increasing number of complex emergencies affecting people and the planet's health, this is a timely book. What is good for the planet's health is good for people's health and vice versa. There are major win-win opportunities; greener often also means healthier. Applying a health lens can help catalyse action in some areas; in others, health gains are a positive side effect. A systemic approach can help maximize impact and save lives.

'We must identify incentives and "tipping points" for positive change, promoting accountability for health consequences—both good and bad—and generating demand for healthy societies. This means encouraging and empowering action from citizens, governments and corporations.

'Healthy life expectancy should be a key measure of success, not merely life expectancy. Well-being rather than merely economic growth should be the leading objective of our societies. All of this is possible.'

Dr Anders Nordström
Ambassador for Global Health, Swedish Ministry
of Foreign Affairs
Acting Director General, WHO (2006)

'Dr Reddy's *Pulse to Planet* is a riveting read and takes one on an exploratory journey from the intricate internal homeostasis of the human body to the planetary determinants of health and disease. In his typical erudite, articulate and highly readable style, he explains why the human race is facing an existential crisis today and what we can do to bring about positive changes. Mainly targeted at the young reader, this book nevertheless is an interesting and educative read for people of any age. It is thought-provoking and provides scientific explanations for common phenomena. Rather than another exposition of a doomsday scenario, this book provides reason for optimism and explains how we can both promote health and well-being as well as protect our planet.'

Dr Soumya Swaminathan
Chairperson, Swaminathan Foundation
Former Chief Scientist, WHO

'Human health is the single biggest driver for change when it comes to environmental management. We act when we understand how poison in our air, water or food is harming our bodies. Today, the additional challenge is to connect the dots of our health, our food with planetary health. The COVID-19 pandemic was a result of our dystopian relationship with nature. That is why this book by Dr K. Srinath Reddy is a must-read. He brings together the knowledge of human health and its connection with nutrition and nature in the book. This is about our common future. We do not have the luxury of good health without the blessings of mother nature.'

Sunita Narain
Director General, Centre for Science and Environment
Editor, *Down To Earth*

'We live in turbulent times, seventy years into the Anthropocene, transgressing six of the nine planetary boundaries and starting to see signs of earth losing resilience, causing social-ecological boomerang effects on humanity across the world. The COVID-19 pandemic was one of these manifestations, and we are in for more surprises in the future. Srinath Reddy provides a chart of how to navigate these increasingly stormy waters. An essential read for anyone interested in safeguarding our future on earth.'

Professor Johan Rockström
Joint Director, Potsdam Institute for Climate Impact Research
Former Director, Stockholm Resilience Centre
Winner of International Cosmos Prize (2015)

'*Pulse to Planet* traverses a vast terrain of factors, from microbiomes to maladapted modernity, which define of our interconnectedness in health. This brilliant landscaping of critical determinants shaping the health of humanity and the planet is written with illuminating precision, parsimony and punch. Harnessing the promise and mitigating the perils of our shared health future is the clarion Dr Reddy issues to next generation leaders. Their odds of rising to the challenge are greatly enhanced by this magnum opus that captures the wisdom of one of the great health leaders of our time.'

Dr Timothy Grant Evans
Director, School of Population and Global Health,
McGill University
Formerly served at WHO and the World Bank

'A hopeful, galvanizing vision for a healthier world. In *Pulse to Planet*, K. Srinath Reddy reminds us that health is fundamentally interconnected and we can only solve the challenges we face—from climate change to global inequality—by working together, led by a rising generation committed to shaping a better future. This book provides a roadmap for these efforts.'

Professor Sandro Galea
Robert A. Knox Professor and Dean,
Boston University School of Public Health
Former Chair of Epidemiology,
Mailman School of Public Health, Columbia University

'Dr Srinath Reddy has beautifully and concretely used "health" to demonstrate what Mahatma Gandhi had once said: "Earth provides enough to satisfy every man's needs, but not every man's greed."

'This book convinces all generations to support the highly motivated and competent new generation to tackle the social and commercial determinants of planetary health. It provides the "wisdom" to enlighten their movements.'

Dr Suwit Wibulpolprasert
Advisor to Ministry of Public Health, Thailand
Winner of WHO's (South-East Asia Region) Hero of Public
Health Award (2023)

'It is a great book, not because it provides new facts but because it is from the lens of an experienced and wise man who brings together the many facets of health, genes, environment, special interests and equity. He manages to unfold the holistic conundrum of health in front of the eyes of future readers. Yes, I fully agree that health is the ultimate summative indicator/measure of sustainable development, and Srinath Reddy brings this masterfully to bear.'

Professor Dr Rainer Sauerborn
Senior Professor, Heidelberg University
Former Head, Institute of Global Health,
Heidelberg University Hospital
Member, Intergovernmental Panel on Climate Change

'In a nutshell, this is honestly one of the very finest "medical" books I have read. I use inverted commas for "medical" because this book is extremely accessible to non-medical practitioners—even while it is based on the deepest, most erudite medical research. Srinath Reddy is, in my opinion, one of the best medical minds—with years of hands-on experience coupled with continuous research to keep abreast of the latest developments in the fast-changing world of medicine. This is a book for all of us, and I recommend it most strongly. It is a must-read.'

Dr Prannoy Roy
Economist, psephologist and political analyst
Former Executive Chairperson, NDTV

'This book is a call to action for young people from one of the foremost experts in health in South Asia. Dr Reddy makes it clear that he is addressing non-experts, the youth, the community and all the stakeholders in health; and yet through this dialogue he is actually speaking to the "experts"—reminding us that those who matter need to be included in all health discourse. It is also an appeal to the "older" generation to recognize the linkages between determinants of health, the planet's health and current actions at the global and national levels. *Pulse to Planet* delivers an emotional call for moral action on health. Based on evidence but recounted in a personally convincing manner, it is a passionate appeal for us to recognize the fundamental intersectionality of our existence as a global community.'

Dr Adnan A. Hyder,
Senior Associate Dean for Research, Professor of Global Health
Director, Center on Commercial Determinants of Health,
Milken Institute School of Public Health,
The George Washington University

'Drawing on his immense career as a clinical and public health leader, Professor Reddy provides a clear and rousing exposition of the importance of understanding our human connectedness—to each other, across our societies and to the planet that nurtures us—to realize the right to health of all people. Professor Reddy's mission is to stimulate young people to understand that health and health equity are not only important of themselves, but indicators of our success in addressing all the crises that threaten human existence and to support their leadership for the transformative change at which older generations have failed.

'This book is an important resource for young people and for our work!'

Dr Kumanan Rasanathan
Executive Director, Alliance for Health Policy and
Systems Research, WHO

'Dr K. Srinath Reddy's book is a compelling read, showcasing his scientific genius, alacrity, compassion and real-life experiences. He presents a blueprint for saving the planet and human health from "civilizational suicide" by capturing every dimension for a paradigm shift. He makes a brilliant diagnosis and prognosis of the crisis, particularly of the environment and human health. Young people constitute a quarter of the global population. The older population should make way and bequeath the legacy of a sustainable planet for them. I am inspired to act. Read it and you will too.'

Poonam Muttreja
Executive Director, Population Foundation of India

'Pulse to Planet details the journey of our planet from its origins to its future through the present. It is a timely book to preserve the planet that is currently in danger of "civilizational suicide". Written in simple, elegant style, the book makes a plea for the preservation of the planet from the perils of disintegration and extinction.'

Suman Kumar
Former Principal, Bluebells School International
Chairperson, Bluebells Educational Society

'Reading this book is nothing short of an insightful journey that takes you through the determinants of health, from the microscopic genetic factors and microbiome to the macroscopic aspects including nutritional and environmental factors, just to name a few. It holistically and eloquently connects the dots of our perceived individual health to the socioeconomic, commercial and healthcare systems that provide an organized perspective to the reader. I believe the youth in 2023, that certainly looks forward to the realization of the 2030 SDGs, can utilize this book to become well-informed leaders of tomorrow. Hopefully in 2051, we will be able to look back at the lessons incorporated as delineated in the book and goals achieved, while working towards the 2060 goals.'

Dr Priyansh Shah
Founder and President, World Youth Heart Federation

'With great pleasure I'd like to encourage the youth of the society to read this well-written book by Dr K Srinath Reddy. The book proves to be a great source of insights in planetary health, it's connection with the youth and throws light on the way forward for the mission of integration of healthcare and environment health.'

Dr Prabhat Jha
President, Medical Students' Association of India (2023)

'This book simplifies the otherwise misunderstood complex interrelationship between humans and the environment from a health and intersectional lens. It conveys everything you need to know to understand the causes and consequences of the issue of climate crises and their connection with other public health and social issues by breaking down the complexities into digestible concepts and through thoroughly researched evidence. It's a must-have book to navigate through tackling arguably the biggest health emergency of the twenty-first century. I congratulate Dr Reddy for writing this book, which has the potential to be a profound toolkit for advocacy for anyone who cares about our planet, irrespective of their educational qualifications and expertise!'

Dr Salman Khan
Director, Standing Committee on Public Health,
International Federation of Medical Students' Associations

PULSE

to

PLANET

THE LONG LIFELINE
OF HUMAN HEALTH

K. Srinath Reddy

HarperCollins *Publishers* India

First published in India by HarperCollins *Publishers* 2023
4th Floor, Tower A, Building No. 10, DLF Cyber City,
DLF Phase II, Gurugram, Haryana – 122002
www.harpercollins.co.in

2 4 6 8 10 9 7 5 3 1

P-ISBN: 978-93-5699-463-8
E-ISBN: 978-93-5699-468-3

Typeset in 11.5/15.2 Adobe Garamond at
Manipal Technologies Limited, Manipal

Printed and bound at
Nutech Print Services - India

FSC
www.fsc.org
MIX
Paper from
responsible sources
FSC® C143748

This book is printed on FSC® certified paper
which ensures responsible forest management.

To the young people of today who have to shape the world
of tomorrow

and

For all those who believe in the oneness of humanity and the
sanctity of life on this planet

Hitopadesha, 1.3.71:
ayam nijah paroveti ganana laghuchetasam
udaracharitanam tu vasudhaiva kutumbhakam

'This is my own and that a stranger'—is the calculation of
the narrow-minded,
For the magnanimous-hearts, however, the entire earth is
but a family.
—The Maha Upanishad

Ancient Mayan Salutation

The Mayan way of greeting a person was to say '*in lak'ech*', meaning 'I'm another you'. The response was to say '*a la k'in*', meaning 'you're another me'.

We are reflected in others, as they are in us. Our lives are connected. Especially in health and well-being.

Contents

Foreword by N.R. Narayana Murthy

An ideal citizen is well-informed of his duty to the society and his role in good public governance in bettering his society. He is an expert in an important field relevant to the society. He has his heart in the right place, has idealism in his genes and is positive-minded. He works hard and smart, is disciplined and strives for the betterment of his nation and the world with every one of his actions. Finally, he is deep-rooted in enduring values. Prof. Srinath Reddy, a well-known cardiologist and India's best-known public health expert, is one such rare citizen of this country. Srinath believes that the only way you can become the global best is by continually working smart and hard every day to become better today than you were yesterday.

I have known Srinath for over twelve years and have, on many occasions, witnessed his leadership from close quarters. He would take up plausibly impossible and aspirational targets. He would inspire his team through his leadership, work hard relentlessly and achieve his goals. No doubt, he earned the plaudits of a vast group of his admirers, of whom I am one. My relationship with him has been illuminated by his deep concern for the health of our citizens and by his unrelenting determination to make public health initiatives in our country a strong force to achieve that objective. A Chinese proverb says that you cannot be a successful shopkeeper unless you can smile easily. I have been an admiring witness to Srinath's amazing smile in the most trying situations in his bid to sell public health to corporate leaders, government bureaucrats and politicians.

I am happy that Srinath has brought together some of his profound ideas to achieve better health for individuals and to strengthen India's efforts in public health and India's commitment to sustainability in this book. This book is very timely and could not have come from a better expert.

Srinath highlights an important point in making this planet and its dwellers healthier and better. He believes that there is a dual responsibility in this task—responsibility of the individual to himself and the society; and the responsibility of the institutions of commerce, of creators of public opinion and of governance in making sure that they make it easy for individuals to fulfil their responsibility. Publilius Syrus, a Syrian philosopher who lived more than 2,000 years ago, wrote that good health and good sense are the two most important blessings in life. Srinath derives legitimacy from Syrus's view that taking care of one's health results in energy, enthusiasm and inclination for hard and smart work to make the nation and the world better. He believes that good sense will reduce an individual's burden on his family members and on the society. He goes further to say that our good sense will ensure that we hand over this planet to our next generation in a better condition than we inherited it from our previous generation.

Jay W. Forrester, the most celebrated father of systems dynamics and the inventor of magnetic core memory, said, 'In complex systems cause and effect are often not closely related in either time or space. The structure of a complex system is not a simple feedback loop where one system state dominates the behaviour. A complex system has a multiplicity of interacting feedback loops. Its internal rates of flow are controlled by nonlinear relationships.' Srinath rightly takes a systems dynamic view of our society with public health as an important variable in that complex system. So Srinath views this complex system through the lens of human health. I agree with him that an individual's health is shaped by the dynamics of interaction among variables like environment, nutrition, agriculture, food systems, tobacco control, urban design and transport, health policy and systems, industrial policy, education, diversity, human rights and sustainable development. He sums up this excellent book with the words: 'The lifeline of human health truly extends from pulse to planet.' Of course, every one of us must read it in full to get deeper insights of the author.

Srinath uses his public health expertise to delineate the various factors of the complex system of living well on our planet to its readers with a special focus on the youth of our country. Using his deep expertise in public health, he exhorts his readers to make their lives healthier, joyful and purposeful. These precepts, he believes, will strengthen the future of our country and this world. They will also make this planet a better place for us to live in and pass it on to our next generation in a condition better than we got it from our parents. Like Srinath, I too believe that this is a sacred duty of every one of us. We cannot shirk this responsibility. Srinath's positivism, hope, confidence and action for this plausible and aspirational marathon rest on the youth of this country and the world. His confidence and hope shine through his words: 'The amalgam of admirable idealism and amazing energy in young persons can be a formidable force for change.' I have enjoyed reading this seminal book. Please turn the page over and start reading!

N.R. Narayana Murthy
Founder and Chairman Emeritus, Infosys Limited
Former Chairman, Public Health Foundation of India

Foreword by Sir Michael Marmot

A handbook for improving the planet and its inhabitants.

In 1900, life expectancy in the world was about thirty-one. In 2019, before the COVID-19 pandemic, it was close to seventy-three. Such improvement is quite astonishing. Why has it happened? And will it continue? The answer to the first question may inform speculation about the second.

A simple answer to the first question is that the world has become a better place to live. But that improvement is unequally distributed. Between countries there are great inequalities in the conditions that lead to good health. Within countries, too, such inequalities lead to great inequalities in health.

How are we to understand the phrase, 'The world has become a better place to live', and why do great inequalities in health persist? I work in a medical school. Large numbers of medical scientists are devoted to understanding basic biological mechanisms underpinning the biology of health and disease. Others are at the frontiers of medical treatment, developing and evaluating therapy for common and rare conditions. Still others are working in the community in primary care of one form or another. Then, there are my colleagues in epidemiology and public health—looking at the distribution of disease in populations, the causes of that distribution and steps that can be taken to improve health. Across the road, there are psychologists who study human behaviour, specialists in early child development and education, economists and political scientists, agricultural specialists and environmental scientists.

Each of these disciplines is highly relevant to understanding health and disease in populations. Indeed, it is not a takeover bid to argue that measures of health and well-being tell us a great deal about how well society is meeting the needs of its members and creating the conditions for them to flourish. To start to answer our question, of the reasons for remarkable global improvements in health, we need to understand how all of these intersect and interact to influence health and disease. A tall order.

A good place to start is this wonderful book by Srinath Reddy. It is well named: *Pulse to Planet*. An understanding of biology is valuable but, by itself, will not explain improvements in health over time or inequalities within and between countries. An understanding of social and environmental determinants of health is vital, but it is helpful to understand how they act on human biology and psychology. Someone thinking about commercial determinants of health may not spend much time thinking about the microbiome. That is their loss. Read the relevant chapter in this book and understand better how food and environment act on the body. Need to think why and how changes in the social and economic environment might change health behaviours? Read the psychology chapter on behaviour change.

The insights gained will help address the second question: the future. The big challenges are the climate emergency, growing inequalities and political and social threats to health and well-being.

Pulse to Planet gives the reader a way to think about how these might influence health. The book stops short of making predictions, rightly in my view. We shouldn't sit back and wait for the movie of the future play out before us. We need to act, and 'we' will depend heavily on the enthusiasm of young people, the target audience for the book. Given the readability of every chapter, it will be a vital handbook for young people wishing to improve life and health on this fragile planet.

Srinath Reddy's life work has been and continues to be on strategies to improve the health of individuals and populations. His grasp of the multiple levels of health and its determinants are well in evidence in this special book. Read it and use the knowledge to work together for a better future for the planet and its inhabitants.

Professor Sir Michael Marmot CH
Director of the UCL Institute of Health Equity,
University College London
Chair of the WHO Commission on the Social
Determinants of Health
Author of *The Health Gap*

Preface

This book is not meant for health experts. It is for everybody who cares about the future of the world, including health professionals. I wrote it especially to inform and assist young persons, who will live in that future but are in danger of being forced to cope with the calamities created by the present models of distorted development. The main driver of the current speeded-up move towards civilizational suicide is a lack of understanding of how the well-being of humans is closely connected, to one another, other occupants of this planet and to our common environment. We cannot provide course corrections unless this inter-dependence is adequately understood and appreciated by humans who are presently driven by ill-conceived individualism that puts them in conflict with the collective well-being of humanity and the sustainability of planetary health. This book looks at human health as the key summative indicator of sustainable global development and highlights the many areas of connectivity that we must recognize and respect if we have to survive and thrive as a species.

In the year in which this book was written (2021–22), much global concern had been voiced about the threats to the environment at COP 26 and COP 27. Human health too has been the dominant theme of media headlines and people's fears, due to the unrelenting threat of COVID-19. Global economy has been sliding down, even as inequalities have been greatly accentuated by the concentration of wealth and power. All of these have been discussed widely in many scholarly books and sharp media commentaries. What I attempt to do in this book is to present a unifying perspective from the viewpoint of one who sees a healthy life as a common aspiration of all people. It is born out of my belief that health is the best summative indicator of sustainable development as it connects many dimensions of human activity.

I have been fortunate in being exposed to many of those dimensions in my life and career. As a physician and cardiologist, I became familiar not only with the clinical presentations of disease but also with the proximate risk factors and their upstream social, economic, environmental and commercial determinants that create the disease. Clinicians who care for and advise patients emphasize that taking care of one's health is an individual responsibility. It is right that they do so while advising on the dos and don'ts of individual behaviour that affect health. However, many of those behaviours are shaped by or constrained by economic, social, environmental, cultural and commercial factors that operate at the societal level. Availability, pricing and marketing of food products are examples. Whether we breathe highly polluted air or fill our lungs with clean air is not entirely a matter of our personal choice. Public health recognizes these connections better than clinical medicine.

As I moved to the arena of public health, I could interact with and gain insights from the many groups working on environment, nutrition, agriculture and food systems, tobacco control, urban design and transport, health policy and systems, universal health coverage, education, gender equity, human rights and other components of sustainable development. As I read and listened, I became increasingly aware of how interconnected and interdependent these are and how an individual's health is shaped by the dynamics of their interaction. The lifeline of human health truly extends from the pulse to the planet.

I have also had the pleasure and privilege of being associated with young people through two youth groups that I helped to found —HRIDAY (Health Related Information Dissemination Amongst Youth) and SHAN (Student Health Action Network). The former means heart and the latter means pride, in Hindi. These groups convened to discuss the pathways and policies by which the health of their generation is enabled or eroded. Their members became informed advocates and enthusiastic campaigners for change. We organized four global youth meets on health around health-friendly policies needed across many sectors, for sustainable development.

The amalgam of admirable idealism and amazing energy in young persons can be a formidable force for change. This book is intended to provide them with a perspective that views sustainable development through the lens of human health. I am greatly inspired by the leadership of young people like Greta Thunberg and Malala Yousufzai. I have seen many others like them at the national and global youth assemblies that HRIDAY and SHAN convened. The voice of Vinisha Umashankar resonated in my ears as she declared at COP26 in Glasgow, 'I am not just a girl from India, I am a girl from Earth'. I have great hope that the young can rescue the world from the many ills that plague our society today. That will ensure a healthier future for all of humanity. As a doctor, I can wish for nothing more.

However, young people cannot do it on their own. Firmly entrenched business and political interests will resist any change that will not serve them well. Fossil fuels, tobacco, unhealthy foods and beverages, extensive logging and mining leading to deforestation and patent-protected high pricing of essential medicines are among the many threats to human health that have powerful vested interests defending them. I have often wondered what kind of a future those focused on narrow ends wish for their own grandchildren and great-grandchildren who cannot lead isolated lives in an unhealthy world.

The generation that is dictating the patterns of economic and social development of the world today has no right to compromise the natural resources that the coming generation needs or to build destructive models of development that are difficult to dismantle or cause irreversible damage. As Thomas (Tom) Paine, American writer and fighter for independence, wrote,[1] 'Every age and generation must be as free to act for itself, *in all cases*, as the ages and generations which preceded it. The vanity and presumption of governing beyond the grave is the most ridiculous and insolent of all tyrannies'. The future generation should not be shackled by the misjudgements and misdeeds of those deciding the fate of the world today.

Unless a majority of global society recognizes the many connections that shape an individual's health and the need for collective action to positively influence the determinants of health, change will not come easily or soon. So, I hope this book will be read by many older people too. They can help the young of today to change the world to create a better future. It is an inter-generational accord that we all must honour.

Why This Book?

'Most rules that you think are written in stone are just societal. You can change the game and really reach for the stars and make the world a better place.'[1]

—SEBASTIAN THRUN

The third decade of the twenty-first century began dismally with a devastating pandemic raging across the world and gloomy forecasts that more would follow unless humanity changes its pattern of reckless ecological disruption. The Secretary General of the United Nations warned that we are 'digging our graves' by not addressing the threat of climate change with the level of urgency and effectiveness that the evolving crisis demands.[2] The Stockholm Resilience Centre (SRC) has described nine planetary boundaries: (1) stratospheric ozone depletion; (2) loss of biosphere integrity (biodiversity loss and extinctions); (3) chemical pollution and the release of novel entities; (4) climate change; (5) ocean acidification; (6) freshwater consumption and global hydrological cycle; (7) land system change; (8) nitrogen and phosphorus flows to the biosphere and (9) oceans and atmospheric aerosol loading. Changes in these, since 1950, have been tracked. Of these nine, five planetary boundaries were crossed by January 2022.[3] In April 2022, scientists from SRC published a report that concluded that the green water boundary is already transgressed. Green water refers to terrestrial precipitation, evaporation and soil moisture.[4]

The nine planetary boundaries are vital for the protection of human health—indeed for the safety of all life forms on earth. By transgressing them, we endanger our health and put lives in peril. The dangers exist for us today but will be even more for the generations to come. Any consideration of human health must recognize these connections and compel us to act rationally and responsibly.

We are told by both public health leaders and statesmen that the children of today will have a shorter life expectancy than their parents if we do not pay heed to the unhealthy practices of food production and marketing that are driving a bulging epidemic of overweight and obesity, even as diet-related cardiovascular diseases, diabetes and cancers are rapidly rising to heap deaths and disability across all regions of the world.

We need to veer away from this rush to perdition, not just to save those whose lives and well-being are at immediate risk but even more so to avoid the sin of shamefully scarring the lives of future generations. Billions who are yet to be born will be the innocent victims of a dark inheritance, even from the time of their conception if the flawed systems that operate now are not fixed fast.

Responsibility to lead the charge to change the direction and dynamics of our development falls primarily on those who are young in the fateful decade of 2021–30. It is not because they have contributed to creating the corrosive models of development we now have, which they certainly have not, but because they are not trapped into compromised acquiescence or inert inaction by the vested interests that hold older generations captive. It is in the idealism and energy of young change-makers that hope for the future lies.

Undoubtedly, there are several well-meaning older adults who wish the world to travel on other tracks but their ability to effect change has been limited, both because the stakes are less for those who have fewer future years to live and also because their present risk-taking ability does not permit them to take bold steps. Most of them are not decision-makers or even decision-shapers. The rudder is not in their hands. If they could effectively change the systems that are perilously propelling society, rather than merely make small changes within those systems, why would we have a world with widening inequalities, rabid religious discord, appalling anti-science movements, acrimonious political polarization, narrow nationalism, violent ethnic conflicts, terrorism that strikes at will and mass migrations that pitilessly toss children from places with unbearable living conditions to locations where they are locked away as unwanted aliens?

Much as my generation has many good people who rail against the injustices and evils of society, and try to do good in our limited ways, we have failed collectively to achieve a course correction in the first two decades of this century. There is not much hope that we will do far better in the third decade. So, we need the young to assert their rights and demand that society do what is right to benefit all.

The penalty for failure to change the course of global development will be disastrous. Climate change, in particular, will have a cascade of harmful consequences. The forces that are propelling climate change are also preparing the flight plan for the arrival of new pandemics and fuelling the surge of non-communicable diseases, obesity and mental health disorders. The term 'syndemic' has been used to describe the interaction and convergence of several epidemics occurring simultaneously.[5] We are witnessing this now. For example, the COVID-19 pandemic has seen the overlap of an infectious disease with the risk-enhancing effect of co-morbidities like diabetes, hypertension and obesity. If we add the social determinants to this mix, the vulnerability of poor populations to an infectious agent is obvious, because of the limited access to efficient health services. So, the interactions between different disease conditions and social conditions create syndemics that cannot be addressed only through siloed insights and segmented responses. We need a root cause response that recasts our models of development.

When I was young, a major concern about the future of humanity related to the threat of nuclear war and annihilation of large parts or all of the human race. Global campaigns were mounted for nuclear disarmament or, at the very least, for effective safeguards that would greatly reduce the risk of accidental or intentional launch of nuclear weapons. Doomsday descriptions were projected of what would be the likely effects of a nuclear Armageddon. An especially powerful book, which strengthened my own opposition to nuclear weapons, was *The Fate of the Earth* by Jonathan Schell. It provided a dark description of what the world would look like after a nuclear war. Schell urged the readers to act without delay to withdraw the threat we now pose to the earth and to ourselves. He warned, in a painful and poignant portraiture, of what the future may hold if we failed to act.

'The alternative is to surrender ourselves to absolute and eternal darkness: a darkness in which no nation, no society, no ideology, no civilisation will remain; in which never again will a child be born; in which never again will human beings appear on earth and there will be no one to remember that they ever did.'[6]

Writing in 1982, Schell was providing a dramatic description of a nuclear winter descending on earth after a nuclear holocaust. That threat has been mitigated a bit since then, though it still poses a major threat to humanity. While nuclear stockpiles continue to exist, and new nuclear powers are birthing belligerently or crouching clandestinely, the threat of a nuclear war appears less imminent now than it did in the second half of the twentieth century. However, we cannot draw even that level of comfort from the pace of climate change.

The target of limiting the rise of global temperature to 1.5 degrees by the year 2100, by itself a concession to the inevitable, seems very difficult to achieve as global action falls far short of the commitments on paper and nations backtrack on those commitments even before the ink of their signatures on consensus declarations fully dries. Jonathan Schell's dystopian description could well be the picture of the world if climate change continues to advance on its present trajectory. Instead of a nuclear winter, the epitaph of humanity may be written by irreversible and irremediable global warming and its effects on human life.

Clearly, we cannot let that happen. There is still time to resurrect a healthy planet and recreate a healthy human society. All right-thinking people must act and the young must lead. That leadership is sprouting across the world. It must grow in strength, by uniting young people across the world to collectively become an irresistible force for change. The support that it needs from older generations, who are more concerned about personal health than that of the planet, may also be forthcoming if the determinants of health are better understood in terms of how individual health is so closely connected to our collective actions that shape the society we live in. I hope this book serves both purposes.

PART I

What Codes Our Biology?

'When we try to pick out anything by itself, we find it hitched to everything else in the universe.'[*]

—JOHN MUIR

---

* Details available at https://vault.sierraclub.org/john_muir_exhibit/writings/misquotes.aspx

Is It All in the Genes?

'A long healthy life is no accident. It begins with good genes, but it also depends on good habits.'[1]

—DAN BUETTNER

Ever since genes were discovered to be the transmitters of heritability, there has been much speculation about the role they play in determining the many biological features of human beings. Debates regarding the relative importance of the genes we inherit and the environment we live in, for shaping our health and determining our susceptibility to a variety of diseases, have dominated medical literature just as the genetic influence on people's behavioural characteristics has been the subject of heated arguments in sociological publications.

While infectious diseases have been viewed as being caused by extrinsic microbial agents, a number of chronic metabolic diseases have been mostly attributed to genetic aberrations. Even while environmental factors have been recognized as causal contributors to such diseases, there has been exuberant optimism that specific gene therapies could modify or cure these diseases once we unravel the human genome.

3

Great Expectations, Reality Check

When the human genome project commenced in the 1980s, it was expected to provide clear and comprehensive insights into the causes of most diseases and open pathways for their prevention and treatment. In the confident prediction of celebrated American scientist Francis Collins in 2003, the newly unravelled genome would be the key to prevention, diagnosis and treatment. He prophesied that it would 'result in a dramatic transformation of the practice of medicine by 2020'.[2]

Collins, who led the project at the National Institutes of Health (NIH) in the United States of America, also forecast, 'The study of the genome will reveal over the next decade the hereditary factors that contribute to virtually all common diseases, including diabetes, cancer, heart disease, mental illness, hypertension and many others'.[3]

Those expectations have been realized only to a limited extent till 2021. Just about 10 per cent of diseases have a clearly identified genetic linkage. Others appear to be driven mostly by varied environmental exposures over a life course. Very few disorders have a structural gene defect. Many, however, have their origins and progression in altered gene expression due to environmental influences. Some disorders may be purely due to the effect of an external factor, like heat stroke, poisoning, birth trauma or an automobile accident. Leaving them aside, gene–environmental interactions do seem to play a role in many of the disorders Collins referred to. However, the role of the environment appears to be far more important than genetic variations in driving these interactions.

Looking at the way these disorders have risen rapidly in numbers and spread globally over the past 100 years, it should convince us that it is indeed the alterations in our living environment, which have driven a surge in the incidence of most of these diseases. Clearly, our genome has not markedly altered over the past three or four generations. Yet the risks and rates of these diseases have risen dramatically.

Many of these diseases have been labelled as 'lifestyle diseases'. It is a misnomer, as living conditions that promote health or create disease are not lifestyle choices of most individuals. They are created by a combination of social, economic, environmental and commercial determinants. As times have changed, so have the nature and scale of these determinants. Even when the gene pool of the population remains unaltered, changes in the determinants have markedly altered the risk of different diseases.

Genes: Disease and Therapy

Of course, it is important to study genetic disorders that cause a variety of diseases. There are four main types of genetic disorders: those associated with single gene inheritance, those linked to multi-factorial genetic inheritance, chromosome abnormalities and mitochondrial genetic inheritance. Among the many single gene disorders are cystic fibrosis, sickle cell anaemia, Marfan syndrome, Tay-Sachs disease, phenylketonuria, Duchenne muscular dystrophy, polycystic kidney disease and familial hypercholesterolemia.

Other disorders may arise from chromosomal defects (such as Down's syndrome) or through mitochondrial genetic inheritance (such as hereditary optic atrophy). The multifactorial or polygenic disorders, far more numerous than the other three categories, are those where many genes may be involved but environmental factors play the most prominent role. Hypertension and Type 2 diabetes are readily recognizable among these.

What is known as 'gene therapy' is in its early stages and presently has a limited repertoire. The safety of such interventions needs to be closely studied. Pharmacological interventions have been developed for the treatment of some genetic disorders. These can be lifesaving.

Some of them can have wider applications beyond the single gene disorders for which they were developed. For example, PCSK9 inhibitors, developed for treating familial hypercholesterolemia, are now being used to lower cholesterol and reduce the risk of heart attacks and strokes in the more common non-familial conditions that cause raised cholesterol.[4] So research on rare genetic disorders can have payoffs beyond the treatment of those afflicted with that specific condition.

Many diseases that have been researched for genetic predictors have come up with several genes, all of which together explain only a small part of the variance between persons and populations with and without the disease. This is true of coronary heart disease and diabetes. Even where some genes appear more prominently associated than others, their effect has been shown to be blunted by prudent diets and physical activity. This is also true for obesity, which is often seen to have a familial predisposition.

Some genes have been associated with more than one disease condition. That is partly explicable when those diseases have common risk factors or pathological pathways. However, such connections are not always seen. The APOE4 gene has been implicated in Alzheimer's disease in Caucasian populations. The prevalence of this APOE4 allele is highest in the Nigerian population, among all the world populations studied. However, among Nigerians, Alzheimer's disease is rare.[5] Other factors may be protective in them or, as is likely, other triggers may be acting in Caucasian populations for the pathology to be initiated or accelerated. The implication of this gene in atherosclerosis suggests a possible common pathway in the Caucasians, in whom elevation of blood cholesterol and other atherogenic lipids is common. When APOE3/4 polymorphisms are reported to be also associated with increased likelihood of severe malaria, explanations become less clear.

A Broader Understanding of the Environmental Role

It is becoming obvious that for diseases caused by several genes (polygenic disorders), environmental triggers play a dominant role. We are now looking beyond tagging genes for all our health problems. In recent decades, we have become more aware of the fact that our genes act in concert with the genes of the trillions of microbes residing within and on the surface of our bodies. This 'microbiome' plays a major role in our health. So, it is not just our genes that matter for our health.

We have also recognized that changes in gene expression are influenced by several environmental factors. The science of epigenetics has grown by leaps and bounds in the past two decades (refer to Chapter 3). Even the NIH, which heralded the identification of the human genome as the disease-conquering breakthrough of science, is now investing heavily in the study of 'social epigenomics' and 'environmental epigenomics'.

Innovative technologies like CRISPR will make it easier to study gene functions and the impact of their structural changes in the future. Gene therapy will also be assessed better for impact and safety. Genetic markers that predict high risk in certain cancers like inherited breast cancer (BRAC 1 and BRAC2 mutations) or colorectal cancers will be useful in guiding clinical management. However, only about 10 per cent of cancers are presently considered to be genetically determined.[6]

Even the genetic patterns among population groups are no longer static. There is a greater admixture of people with increased mobility, with inter-racial marriages on the rise. Amidst a decrease in consanguinity and departure from inbreeding practices among hitherto confined populations, we see a much greater mixing of genes. When this happens against a background of changing environments and altered living habits, the scope and scale of gene-environmental interactions increases markedly.

So, we recognize that people are connected among themselves and to their living and non-living environments. These relationships affect the health of individuals and populations. Very few lead solitary lives as hermits. They too have to interact with their environment, if not with other people. The subsequent chapters of this book will describe several determinants of health, which we must collectively influence in order to create a healthy future for humanity.

Environment Fine-tunes Our Biology

'If anything is sacred, the human body is sacred.'[1]

—WALT WHITMAN

The famous seventeenth-century French philosopher René Descartes perceived the human body as a machine, composed of multiple parts that are functionally distinct but coordinated for the overall activity and survival of the person.[2] Cartesian reductionism influences the practice of modern medicine even now because the pathology of disease is often studied organ-wise. However, the study of human physiology teaches us how structurally intricate and functionally integrated our organ systems are and how dynamically influenced their activity is by feedback loops that operate at multiple levels. These functions are greatly influenced by our physical environment and living habits. Indeed, the evolution of human physiology, like that of other animals, is shaped by constant adaptation to the environment.

As a medical student, and later as a doctor, I have experienced constant wonderment at the exquisitely designed control systems that guide the human body's functions—both in a steady state and

9

when challenged by a change in the environment. Scientific research continues to unravel fresh facts and provide new insights that tell us how elegantly the human body has been configured for form and function. From connected bodily systems to organs to tissues to cells to subcellular components to transmitter chemicals to circulating hormones (and their receptors) to electrical signals, the body is an amazingly configured and efficiently coordinated unit. For survival, it combines functional stability with dynamic adaptability. It is such a pity that we damage or destroy this wonder of nature with dissolute living or deadly violence.

The way in which the body harmonizes the functions of various internal systems to maintain functional stability is called homeostasis. This is a self-regulatory process in which a dynamic equilibrium is attained through constant calibration and change, which seeks to maintain stability. The French scientist Claude Bernard called it the 'milieu interieur'.[3] Walter Cannon called it 'homeostasis'.[4] He described it as the processes that maintain the internal stability of the body while responding to changes in external stimuli. Homeostasis involves multiple forward and backward loops that can be influenced by higher centres. It is a dynamic process that changes many internal settings to achieve a safe equilibrium that assures physical safety and functional stability with minimal deviation from the optimal physiological state.

Allostasis: Being Stable by Being Variable

Homeostasis became the cardinal tenet of human physiology and the rationale of the body's adaptive and stabilizing responses revolved around it. But how about the environment to which we are responding? That keeps changing. Do we only respond reactively through homeostatic responses or anticipate change and have our body systems prepare proactively to meet that change to avoid instability?

This question brought in the concept of 'allostasis', a term coined by Peter Sterling and Joseph Eyer in 1988.[5] It means being stable by being variable. Think of it as being stable by adjusting your pace when walking on a treadmill as it picks up speed or slows down. This change of speed is anticipated and we prepare our body to respond accordingly.

Allostasis demands that each sensor in the body, of the multitude of regulatory systems, recognize and anticipate the change in demand and prepare each of the expected response mechanisms to adjust its output to meet that demand. Allostasis is achieved through the hormonal axis that links the hypothalamus, pituitary gland and adrenal glands—the autonomic nervous system and the fast reactive cytokine defences of the immune system. To help the body maintain stability, allostasis provides a short-term anticipatory response to variability in the environment. Some have argued that allostasis is a concept embedded in, and not distinct from, homeostasis.

The concept of homeostasis, even with the extended component of allostasis, assumes that the human body is responding to changes that are occurring inside the body (due to disease processes) or outside the body (due to a changing environment). But what about humans changing the internal or external environment through their own actions? Like smoking or chewing tobacco or accelerating global warming through profligate use of fossil fuels. Can we reset our behaviours and shape our environment in a manner that does not cause an allostatic overload that wears down our bodies? For that we must respect both our bodies and our environment.

Human Physiology Displays Nature's Genius

So, spare a thought for the way nature has crafted our body's physiologic systems. A few of those exquisitely configured systems will serve to illustrate the efficient way in which the body seeks to maintain balance and protect health. Each one of them functions with a cascade of controls, feedback loops, resets and reinforcements to achieve overall balance and stability.

Since COVID-19 has been the dominant theme of recent years, let us look at the immune system first. The ensemble cast includes: rapidly mobilized cytokines as the first responders to a microbial threat, antibodies secreted by the B lymphocytes, which combat the virus circulating in the bloodstream, killer and helper T lymphocytes that provide cellular immunity, memory B and T cells and a diverse population of neutrophils.[6] Some of them play a major role in innate immunity, others in acquired immunity, while some feature in both.

The best of modern military strategists will be unable to match the speed of mobilization and efficiency of coordinated deployment that the various components of the immune system display in the defence of our body. Yet, we hamper those defences by weakening our immunity by consuming unhealthy diets, alcohol and tobacco, and depriving the body of sleep, sunlight, adequate physical exercise and clean air.

Think of how our body manages the balance of food intake and glucose regulation. Our appetite is stimulated by the hormone ghrelin (hunger hormone) that is secreted by the stomach and a part of the hypothalamus in the brain. It is short-acting and triggered by the brain's recognition of the need for energy replenishment. As food passes into the small intestine, the brain is signalled again. The satiety hormone leptin is then secreted by the small intestine and adipose tissue of the body. That suppresses the appetite.

It is not surprising that both platelet activator and inhibitor are derived from a common parentage—the cell signalling molecular family of eicosanoids that are derived from polyunsaturated fatty acids. Fine tuning of the balance between clotting and bleeding can, thus, be efficiently managed by the body till we distort the balance through our behaviours. It is also worth noting that the sub-families of eicosanoids are also involved in the regulation of blood pressure, inflammation, allergy, fever, regulation of childbirth, and cell growth. Isn't it remarkable as to how so many of our body's functions are so well coordinated through interlinked regulatory systems? The genius of nature is amazing, in terms of the connectivity it provides within our bodies and to the nature outside. This is an orchestra that will make beautiful music for our health, till we strike the wrong keys or sing discordant notes.

As the digested food releases glucose, which passes the blood–brain barrier, the body modulates the blood levels of glucose that is needed as fuel by the body's cells. Insulin is secreted by the beta cells of pancreas and lowers blood glucose by enabling glucose to enter the cells for utilization. The alpha cells, also in the pancreas, secrete glucagon, when blood sugar goes down. This hormone helps to raise blood sugar levels by converting glycogen stored in the liver to glucose (glycogenolysis) and amino acids from proteins into glucose (gluconeogenesis). Glucagon secretion is stimulated by low blood sugar levels, protein-rich meals and adrenaline. Its secretion is reduced by carbohydrate-rich meals.

The food that passes from the stomach to the small intestine is not just a speeding sugar express. It contains many other components that influence the speed and level of nutrient absorption, satiety and the rate of blood sugar rise. It carries the nutrients we need and those that our gut bacteria relish. Proteins, fat and fibre (soluble and insoluble) play a role in these processes. They are dealt with by different enzymes and evoke several other physiological effects than sugars do.

Our body deals with all that complexity without us being aware of it. The brain silently monitors these processes through its sensors and ensures order through its neuro-hormonal controls and feedback loops. Yet, even the rational part of the brain succumbs to temptations of unhealthy foods, which increase the level of dopamine (the 'pleasure hormone') in our brain.

This pleasure creates a craving for foods rich in sugar, fat and salt, and overrides the signals of satiety. The manufacturers and marketers of unhealthy food products and beverages exploit this chink in the rational armour of our brain. Obesity and related diseases are not because our physiology has failed us. It is because sections of the food industry have found a trojan horse to breach its defences.

A life-threatening manifestation of COVID-19 has been the increased tendency for blood clots to form in both arteries and veins. When we examine the mechanisms related to the clotting of blood, we again see a balance of forces that cause or prevent it in our body. There are two pathways to initiate blood clots. One proceeds through a set of circulating blood proteins produced by the liver. These coagulation factors, when activated, end with a fibrin mesh that traps the blood cells and creates a clot. The other pathway is via blood cells called platelets. When activated, the platelets produce a chemical called thromboxane A2. This stimulates clotting.

Another chemical called prostacyclin, generated by the blood vessel wall, prevents clotting by countering the action of thromboxane A2. Both these chemicals are generated from a common precursor, the eicosanoids lipids (prostaglandins), and are structurally very similar. This yin and yang of coagulation is another fascinating reminder of how delicately the body creates a balance to keep us alive and healthy. Unfortunately, we disturb that balance when we eat foods that have loads of unhealthy fats or smoke or become very sedentary.

Consider the way the strength and suppleness of the bones in our body is regulated. Calcium levels in our blood are elevated by the action of the parathyroid hormone secreted by the parathyroid gland that adjoins the thyroid gland in the front of our neck. The calcium helps bone formation, which is engineered by cells called the osteoblasts. When osteoblasts are surrounded by their secretions, they are called osteocytes. These make a hormone called sclerostin that inhibits bone formation. Sclerostin acts as a mechanosensor. When osteocytes sense bone-loading activities performed by a person, sclerostin secretion is reduced. This helps in stress-bearing bone formation. The calcium levels in the blood are lowered by a hormone called calcitonin; it is secreted by the thyroid gland. Calcitonin acts to reduce the activity of osteoclasts that break down the bone, so that the blood calcium levels do not increase too much. But osteoclasts serve a very important function in normal conditions. They eat the bone, to reshape it into a stronger and more resilient structure that is better at bearing loads than before.

This constant remodelling goes on, with the osteoblasts laying the bone like masons and osteoclasts reshaping it like carpenters chipping away, with the parathyroid hormone and calcitonin helping by correctly rationing the calcium supply. How do the osteoblasts and osteoclasts know how much bone to lay and how to reshape it? They get their signals from piezoelectric currents generated by bone stress. Every time you twist or turn in a chair or in a dance, those signals go to these bone-sculpting cells! We do them no favour when we adopt wrong postures in office chairs, in vehicles or pour over computers and cell phones for long periods. Also, when we are sedentary, we do not give our bones the stimulus to stay strong. Our nutrition and physical activity determine our bone health. Apart from personal choices, our social conditions determine our diets and the levels of physical activity. The living conditions we create in a changing society reflect on our individual bodies.

Environment Shapes Health

If we want to marvel further at the amazingly intricate and extraordinarily efficient interconnected mechanisms of our body's functioning, we need only to look at the brain and nervous system. As Lisa Feldman Barrett in her brilliant book, *Seven and a Half Lessons*

About the Brain (2020)[7] explains, the brain has evolved to perform a wide range of recognition, regulatory and executive functions with a speed and efficiency unmatched by any single human invention so far. With 'tuning' and 'pruning' of its neurons, the brain evolves over our lifetime to keep us healthy and out of danger.

Feldman Barrett also remarks that the best thing as well as the worst thing for your nervous system is another human. Here is what she says about the biological and emotional connections that are part of our social existence: 'Most people eat food farmed by others. Many live in homes built by others. Our nervous systems are tended by others. Your brain secretly works with other brains. This hidden cooperation keeps us healthy, so it matters how we treat each other in a very real, brain-wiring way.'

The above examples are but a few of the many areas where human physiology has been superbly designed through years of evolutionary responses to our environment and refinements made to accommodate even our daily habits. It is truly amazing to find the pairs of seemingly opposing influences closeted close by, using sensors to decide how much each must contribute to maintain a healthy balance, be it blood sugar or bone strength. This kind of magic is seen everywhere, from the sophisticated networks of the nervous system to the regulation of our skin temperature.

However, the human body does not exist in a vacuum. It functions in physical and social environments that provide the surroundings and stimuli to challenge our physiological responses and reset them, to maintain homeostasis with minimal drift from a steady state and accommodate anticipatory allostatic adjustments to expected changes in the environment. While maintaining harmony with our environment, we need to proactively shape it so that it supports and secures our good health. Our environment shapes our health. We should shape our environment so that it is most favourable to our health, both individually and as a human collective.

'I, Me, Myself'? Not Really!

> 'The role of the infinitely small in nature is infinitely great.'[1]
>
> —LOUIS PASTEUR

Till recently, it was only a member of royalty who could refer to himself or herself in the plural 'we' instead of I. Not even persons with a multiple personality disorder would do that. Now it is clear that every human being can use the royal 'we'. It is not a universal assertion of the democratic spirit or a republican rejection of royal privilege. It is just that human beings are now known to be minority shareholders in their own bodies, far outnumbered by other living organisms that cohabit and profoundly influence what happens to our bodies.

First, a lesson in humility. For far too long, human beings have been obsessed with the notion that they are the pinnacle of evolution and the acme of civilization. This feeling led to the belief that each individual human is biologically complete and capable of functioning independently of other living forms, which were considered subsidiary. Even the care and concern for them rose from economic, ethical or emotional reasons rather than a feeling that humans are biologically dependent on them.

Whether used for food, labour, sport, entertainment or pleasure through petting, there was no sense of shared identity with the 'other' living forms. The use of the first person singular as an identity (I, me, myself) conveyed that distinctive imagery of an independent individual. Grammatically correct but, as it turns out, biologically wrong.

What Is a Microbiome?

In popular perception, microbes featured in the worst category of the 'others' and are regarded as disease-causing villains that need to be hunted and destroyed. 'Eliminate' or 'eradicate' are militaristic terms used for disease control programmes directed at harmful microbes. While strong action against pathogenic microbes is certainly needed, paranoia has shaped the popular perception of all microbes as dreadful germs. The hygiene hypothesis, assiduously advanced by science and aggressively marketed by commercial advertisements urging us to 'kill those bugs', did not help us make a distinction between friends and foes in the vast world of microbes.

Science again, over the past two decades, has brought us a deluge of new information and provided astounding insights into the intimate relationship between human beings and a galaxy of microbes, which are integral to the composition and functioning of the human body. These are now graced with the collective name of the microbiome, conferred by Nobel Laureate Joshua Lederberg,[2] who had earlier unravelled the intricacies of bacterial genetics but later became concerned over the indiscriminate demonization of all microbes as a menace to be decimated.[3] Far from being regarded as dreaded enemies, many of the constituents of the microbiome are now seen as essential for human growth and survival. Disturbances, in the crowded cosmos of microbes that is our constant companion, are being associated with a diversity of health disorders.

It comes as a bit of a shock when we are told that each of us is only 43 per cent human, the rest of the cells in 'our body' come from the microbiome that exists in teeming trillions on our skin, in our gut, mouth, airways, urogenital tract and secretions such as breast milk.[4, 5] Their genes far outnumber those of humans. In contrast to the 22,000 human genes, the gut microbiota alone have about 3.3 million genes.[6] Overall, of the panoply of genes that we carry in our bodies, only 1 per cent are truly human genes.

Just imagine all of these gene factories functioning in our body. We will then realize that it is the combined effects of our genes and 'their' genes that determine our lives. What is more humbling is that while human beings are 99.9 per cent identical to each other in their genome profiles, the microbiomes can vary up to 80–90 per cent between their human hosts.[7] So, our identity is mainly forged by the microbes who are our tenants, even though the nameplate is ours!

The resident microbiome helps to boost the body's immunity, fight off harmful invaders from the external microbial horde, digest otherwise indigestible food components, promote healthy growth and prevent many health disorders. The role of the microbiome as a prime defender against deadly diseases came to prominence when it was reported that 'faecal transplants', from healthy persons into the large bowel of persons with life-threatening diarrhoea from a bacterium called *Clostridium difficile*, were dramatically effective in saving lives. This form of treatment, now more politely called 'microbiota transfer therapy' (MTT),[8] is opening up research into the understanding and treatment of many disorders that even till a few years ago would never have been associated with a murky microbial milieu.

Mother and the Microbiome

The protective armour of the microbiome is acquired at birth itself, as the baby passes through the birth canal of the mother. The vaginal microbiota coat the skin and scalp of the new born to provide the first line of defence against the threat of infection that lurks in the external world. Children born through caesarean section miss this first gift wrapping of microbiota that the mother provides her precious baby with. Such children appear to be more prone to allergic and autoimmune disorders such as asthma, Type 1 diabetes, juvenile arthritis, connective tissue disorders and inflammatory bowel disease as they grow up.[9]

Trials are on to test if coatings of vaginal secretions (vaginal seeding)[10] provided to a caesarean baby after the birth have a substantially protective effect that compensates for the missed opportunity. Breastfeeding seems to quickly provide an additional channel for early transfer of the maternal microbiome to the newborn and the growing infant. This is through the breast milk as well as the intimacy of skin contact with the mother. Even the caesarean baby gains early protection from breastfeeding, which must continue for as long as possible both for nutritional reasons and for building up the infant's microbiome. Interestingly, the composition of the microbiome changes during pregnancy, with a bacterial species called the bifidobacteria proliferating in response to the maternal hormone progesterone in late pregnancy. This seems to be an evolutionary response in anticipation of childbirth.

Mother's milk is also intriguingly related to the nutrition of the infant's gut microbiome. Maternal breast milk contains a type of sugar known as oligosaccharides. These are indigestible for the infant and cannot be used for its own nutrition but the gut microbiome thrives on it. This is especially true of the bifidobacteria that, as we have noted, proliferate during the late pregnancy and are passed on to the child at birth.[11] The microbiome, in turn, fosters infant nutrition by helping in the manufacture of some key nutrients such as vitamins while also maintaining gut immunity. A malnourished mother from a poor family, is likely to be deficient in these oligosaccharides. Her infant will have a deficient microbiome as a result and become malnourished as well.

Recent evidence also indicates that the microbiome plays a role even in women's fertility. Till late twentieth century the uterine cavity was considered to be sterile. Later research revealed the presence and composition of the microbiome throughout the female reproductive tract. Several studies indicated the dominance of the *Lactobacillus* species in the healthy uterine microbiome. The presence of microorganisms such as *Gardnerella vaginalis* was associated with unsuccessful in-vitro fertilization, embryo implantation failure and miscarriage. The microbial signatures appear to be different in persons who become pregnant, do not become pregnant or miscarry.[12, 13]

Cathryn Nagler from the University of Chicago[14] describes healthy microbiota as 'gut peacemakers'. Her research group believes that neonatal colonization with a clostridial species of bacteria protects against food allergies. They found that germ-free mice were protected against allergic reaction to cow milk protein when given bacteria from healthy infants but not when they were given bacteria from infants who had cow milk allergy. The survival advantages conferred by an inter-generational transfer of such protective bacteria appear to be a remarkable feature of our evolution as part of a larger ecosystem and not merely as a standalone species. Nagler is concerned that by markedly altering our food habits, such as by consuming ultra-processed and low fibre foods, we may have changed the nature of food available to the bacteria within us, making them less capable of protecting us from allergic and inflammatory disorders.

Have we drugged or poisoned our own security guards?

Environment and Behaviours Mould the Microbiome

The microbiome is acquired at birth and grows with maternal contact and breastfeeding in early infancy but is not static thereafter. It grows and changes through contact with its surroundings—both animate and inanimate—as the many new varieties of microbes that aim to enter the body are accommodated or rejected. From contact with pets to exposure to dust and dirt, the sources of new microbial acquisition can be many. Non-pathogenic microbes can expand the microbiome, in numbers and diversity, making it a stronger ally to human development and health. Each individual develops a distinctive microbiome much like our unique fingerprints but the profile of the microbiome changes over the lifetime in response to the external and internal environments, unlike the fingerprints.

The microbiome is also altered by our behaviours. The diet we consume has an effect on the composition of the microbiome, by encouraging or inhibiting the growth of certain species. It was seen that malnourished children (and mice) in Bangladesh and Malawi have a limited microbiome that responds not only to MTT from well-nourished children but also to interventions with diverse diets.[15]

Exercise too has been shown to alter the microbiome. Some of the beneficial effects of prudent diets and exercise, in reducing inflammatory biomarkers in the body and promoting a healthy metabolic profile, appear to be related to the changing composition of the microbiome.

The tenets of Ayurveda emphasize the relationship of an individual's specific dietary proclivities and behaviour of the digestive tract as predictors of health and disease. Other traditional systems too place a high premium on customizing dietary prescriptions to specific health disorders. They seem to be supported by the growing science of the microbiome. If our health is indeed greatly influenced by the dietary preferences of our resident microbiome, should our future choices from an à la carte menu in a restaurant be dictated more by the taste of our gut microbes than by the preferences of our palate? And how will we know that? The future may reveal the scientific tools by which we may plan our diets to meet the requirements of a healthy microbiome. For now, we can only wonder at the manner in which the interdependence of human behaviours and the functions of the microbiome appears to shape our health.

Microbiome and the Connection to Various Diseases

Apart from child undernutrition, alterations in the microbiome have also been linked to obesity, through hormonal and inflammatory pathways. *Helicobacter pylori* resides in our gut and is involved in signalling hunger or satiety to the brain. By regulating acid secretion in the stomach, this bacterium causes a decrease in ghrelin, a hormone that regulates appetite. Absence of this microbe in the stomach elevates the level of ghrelin, which in turn increases the appetite, leading to excess consumption of food and obesity.[16] Consumption of high fat diets reduces the microbiome volume, while favouring the growth of bacteria that stimulate fat deposition. Different results are observed when sterile mice, made germ-free by antibiotics, have faecal transplants from obese or slim mice. In the former case, the recipients develop obesity, compared to the latter who remain non-obese.

The integrity of the epithelial lining of the intestines seems to be dependent on the protection provided by the gut microbiome. The resident 'friendly' microbiome induces tolerance in the gut endothelium and participates in promoting gut immunity, endothelial stability and gut–brain interaction, while helping to keep out pathogenic bacteria. Alterations in the microbiome (dysbiosis) are associated with a variety of gastrointestinal disorders such as inflammatory bowel disease, celiac disease, antibiotic-induced colitis and oesophagitis. Such disturbances may also be involved in carcinogenesis.

Much more unexpected is the growing evidence of the involvement of the microbiome in neuropsychiatric disorders such as depression, autism, Alzheimer's, dementia, Parkinson's and schizophrenia.[17] While it seems farfetched to think that that brain is affected by changes in the microbiome, recent research is pointing in that direction. Usually, the brain is protected from the direct invasion of microbes by the blood–brain barrier. However, the microbiome can still influence the brain through its effects on nutrients, hormones and various metabolites. The microbes can also gain entry from the nose, climbing up the nerve endings of the olfactory nerve, which is responsible for our sense of smell. Metabolites released by the gut microbiome act on the nerve endings of the vagus nerve that abound in the gut. These signals can be transmitted to the brain.

The amyloid protein has long been linked to Alzheimer's disease as a key manifestation of brain pathology. The accumulation of amyloid and tau proteins became the hallmark of this disorder, which is the leading cause of dementia. Trials to target the amyloid with drugs have, however, proved to be disappointing failures. Coincidentally, the discovery that amyloid has potent anti-microbial properties led to the speculation that the amyloid deposition is a response of the brain to protect itself from microbes, which unfortunately results in self-harm in terms of severe cognitive decline.

Microbiome patterns among persons with Alzheimer's disease have been shown to have lower levels of butyrate-producing bacteria and reduction in the expression of P-Glycoprotein, a critical mediator of intestinal epithelial homeostasis.[18] In other words, the lining of the intestine loses its ability to maintain its integrity. The net result of this disturbance is a reduction in anti-inflammatory microbes and mediators, and an increase in pro-inflammatory microbes. This pattern was observed in contrast to persons without dementia or other forms of dementia. The inflammatory state seems to lead to brain pathology through the gut–brain axis. A systemic inflammatory state and a breach in the intestinal mucosal barrier due to changes in the microbiota can lead to the brain becoming vulnerable to inflammatory metabolites and even a breach in the blood–brain barrier. These can affect the nature of immune response in the brain and brain cell function.

Two types of gut bacteria, which thrive on a ketogenic diet, may provide benefits in controlling epilepsy. This they may do by providing their human hosts with neurotransmitters that interrupt the type of electrical activity in the brain, which is associated with seizures. A strain of bacteria has also been shown to provoke symptoms of Parkinsonism in mice. Behavioural disorders, such as depression and autism, too are being linked to the microbiome.[19] Faecal transplants, from humans with depression into previously active mice, have been shown to induce inactivity and social withdrawal in those animals.[20] A high fat diet too had similar effects. However, when the microbiome was enriched with certain bacterial species, such as *Lactobacillus reuteri*, the animals became active and social again.

Microbiome-induced vagus nerve signals, from the gut to the brain, can alter the production of brain hormones. Oxytocin is a hormone that promotes social bonds. When the production of that hormone is diminished, reclusive social behaviours emerge. Structural changes too can occur in the brain due to the metabolic effects of the microbiome. They appear to be particularly profound during pregnancy and birth, as the metabolites from the mother's microbiome travel to the growing foetal brain. The growing infant microbiome, seeded at and after birth by the mother and the environment, also affects the rapidly growing brain of the child. Scientists like Rebecca Knickmeyer are studying the relationship of low-diversity microbiomes of infants to the connections between different brain structures and the amygdala, which is the emotion processing area of the brain.[21, 22] As emotions and behaviours increasingly get linked to changes in the gut microbiome and its metabolites, the phrase 'gut feeling' may acquire an entirely new meaning!

A recent study in persons affected by COVID-19 has shown a disturbed microbiome, with low microbial diversity. The viral infection itself and inappropriate use of antibiotics appear to be contributors to such an altered composition of the gut microbiota. Antibiotic-resistant microbes had also migrated to the blood stream in 20 per cent of the patients. The study showed that the COVID-19 virus infection damages the gut microbiome, even in the absence of antibiotic use.[23] Since the relationship of gut microbiome to inflammatory process in the body is well established, this study indicates yet another pathway by which COVID-19 can cause severe disease and death.[24]

Apart from drugs like antibiotics altering our microbiome, the levels at which many orally ingested medicines become available within the body (bioavailability) too are altering the gut microbiota. Drug transport processes in the intestine are affected and gastrointestinal properties are altered, which can decrease or increase drug bioavailability and also influence interactions between different drugs. Microbial enzyme activity is responsible for such changes. The relationship of several drugs and the microbiome may be bidirectional, each altering the other.

Future pharmacological management of several diseases will have to take into account such interactions, while personalizing prescriptions and monitoring the effects of treatment. Interestingly, examination of the physical characteristics of a patient's stool, before and after initiation of treatment, has been a feature of traditional Indian systems of medicine like Ayurveda. With modern scientific methods, we should be able to assess and monitor the relationship and response of the gut microbiome to different drugs. As often happens when a new pathway of scientific discovery opens up, there is great excitement about the microbiome and much enthusiasm for exploring its links to many diseases. From obesity, atherosclerosis and cardiovascular disease to rheumatoid arthritis, asthma, diabetes and cancers, there is a rush of research initiatives seeking such connections. These are early days yet to draw firm conclusions with regard to most of the disorders that are being associated with disturbances in the microbiome. However, it is likely that this is a fast-developing area and many new concepts may emerge about the key role of the microbiome in human health.

Want to Live Long? Take Care of Your Microbiome

In July 2021, Japanese researchers found[25] that people who lived beyond their 100th birthday (Japan has so many of them) had a larger number of the types of gut bacteria that produce chemicals which could prevent or fight serious infections. These chemicals, which are secondary bile acids, especially one called isoallo-lithocholic acid, could keep dangerous bacteria like *C. difficile* and vancomycin-resistant *Enterococcus* from growing or replicating. Protection against life-limiting infections might be only one of the several mechanisms by which the microbiome can gift us a long and healthy life.

Even at this stage, it is clear that the microbiome has co-evolved with us and is an integral part of our 'self'. We coexist! We are connected! What evolution has united, let no silos of species science tear asunder.

Gene Expression Is Epigenetically Modulated throughout Life

'Epigenetics doesn't change the genetic code, it changes how that's read. Perfectly normal genes can result in cancer or death. Vice-versa, in the right environment, mutant genes won't be expressed. Genes are equivalent to blueprints; epigenetics is the contractor. They change the assembly, the structure.'[1]

—BRUCE LIPTON

How does a fertilized ovum start with a set of genes, which subsequently shape the human body into different organs with distinctive functions? How does the environment, whether in the mother's womb or later in the food, air and water that our body thrives on, change the way our genes express themselves? What happens to gene expression if we smoke tobacco, for instance?

Those who believe that life is forever determined by the genes we inherit must consider these questions. If they do, they will discover the fascinating science of epigenomics (also called epigenetics). While the gene structure remains unchanged, gene expression is subject to dynamic alterations in response to the many needs of the body throughout a lifetime and the many influences of the environment in which we function.

How Is Gene Expression Altered?

Think of music from a piano. The keys of a piano are the same but the music that is made varies according to the notations and the tonal quality depends on whose fingers are on the keys and what type of music is being played. Epigenetic influences play the piano on the keys that are our genes.

How does this happen? Even as research continues to unravel these mechanisms, there are three major pathways of epigenetic modulation: DNA methylation, histone modification and non-coding RNA. None of these change the basic structure of the genes but each of these can regulate the gene function. This can be 'up regulation' or 'down regulation'.

In DNA methylation,[2] a chemical group is added to the DNA. The addition of this methyl group occurs at the point where it can block the proteins that attach to the gene to gain instructions from it. Methylation 'turns off' the gene and reduces its functional effects. Removal of the chemical group, by the process of demethylation, 'turns on' the gene and activates its functions.

Histone modification[3] does not alter the DNA but affects the proteins (histones) around which the DNA is wrapped. If the DNA is tightly wrapped around the histones, proteins that are meant to get instructions from the DNA cannot 'read' the DNA. The gene is 'turned off'. Genes that are not wrapped around the histones are 'turned on' and can express themselves. Chemical groups can be added or removed from the histones, altering the gene function. Histone acetylation and de-acetylation are processes that affect gene function. Histone modification is involved in many regulatory stages of gene function.

Ribonucleic acid (RNA) occurs as coding RNA and non-coding RNA. Both forms are made through instructions from the DNA. The coding RNA carries the instructions for making specific proteins that in turn regulate the body functions. Non-coding RNA attaches to the coding RNA, preventing it from carrying its protein-making functions. The functions of the coding RNA can be 'down' or 'up' regulated depending on whether or not it is tagged by non-coding RNA.

How Do Epigenetic Responses Adapt to a Changing Environment?

All of this would be interesting enough if this was just an internal arrangement of the body's physiology. However, the body constantly depends on and has to respond to changing external inputs. If we had genes that played the same musical theme over and over again, without responding to changing audience demands and tastes, we would never get on with life. So, epigenetic mechanisms step into managing the gene expression and it is the impact of their function as best suited to different circumstances that we encounter.[4]

Regulation of the way proteins are produced in cells helps in cell differentiation to perform varied functions in the body. They steer the formation and function of bone cells as distinct from muscle cells and the latter as distinct from nerve cells. These cells produce different proteins. Muscle cells do not produce proteins that are required for bone growth or brain function.

Environmental influences such as the diet we consume or exposure to pollutants can alter epigenetic impacts on gene expression.[5] As the foetus developing in the womb or the child in the early years of life experiences undernutrition, epigenetics change the programme of the body's metabolism to spare the limited nutrition available for the growth of the brain and nervous system, as survival depends on brain function. Other organs shrink in size and the lean muscle mass develops insulin resistance to spare glucose for the brain. As the child grows, this metabolic programming through epigenetic controls becomes counterproductive when there is an increase in dietary intake. Diabetes and cardiovascular disease manifest in early adulthood. A small lung size reduces the respiratory capacity for exercise and loads the dice against survival when severe respiratory infections strike.

Air pollution modulates DNA methylation, usually lowering it. Those changes lead to inflammation of various body tissues and diseases of different organs. Blood vessels are typically affected, leading to heart attacks and brain strokes. Lungs are also damaged by the inflammatory response to constant assaults by pollutants such as particulate matter, black carbon, ozone, nitrogen oxides and polyaromatic hydrocarbons. Prolonged stress too has been observed to induce harmful epigenetic effects.

Epigenetic Changes Are Heritable and Alterable

Epigenetic influences can also be inherited. Environmental exposures can strongly imprint epigenetic modifications that may be passed on to the offspring.[6] This is particularly worrisome when epigenetic changes occur due to adverse nutritional or environmental exposures in a pregnant woman who is carrying a female foetus. It affects not only the woman and the foetus in the womb but the ova (egg cells) in the ovaries from which the foetus is developing. Thus, three generations can be affected by a powerful environmental exposure that has detrimental effects on the body.

However, epigenetic influences can change over the lifetime, if a healthy environment alters the epigenetic stimulus. While research is still gathering evidence on the nature of health-promoting stimuli and the duration of their protective effect, our best bet lies in ensuring healthy diets to all across their life course, creating pollution-free environments and reducing conflicts and inequities that create and perpetuate stress. These are not in the hands of the individual alone. Societal changes, such as these, require communities and countries to cooperate to create conducive environments and supportive social systems. Humans need to connect with each other to embrace this vision and convert it into reality.

The microbiome too plays a major role in steering epigenetic influences. Metabolites produced by the gut microbiota can regulate epigenetic modifications. As the nature of diet influences the microbiome, a change in the metabolites produced by altered gut flora may be mediating epigenetic changes that can lead to obesity, diabetes and cardiovascular diseases. The interaction between our genes (inherited), microbiota (changing with our diets) and environmental triggers that activate epigenetic changes is an area of scientific enquiry that is likely to reveal much more than we know now about the pathways of disease and the protective practices that promote health. While we cannot change the genes of the 8 billion individuals who now populate the earth, we can create a social and environmental milieu that makes these interactions favourable to human health across generations.

Expanding Frontiers

New areas of academic research and knowledge application are emerging, which extend our knowledge of the biological pathways of epigenetic modulation to the broader societal drivers of such processes. 'Environmental Epigenomics' and 'Social Epigenomics' are among these. By advancing our understanding of gene–environmental interactions and their social drivers, epigenomics is opening up a vast arena of action for social changes that can protect and promote health. An epigenetic change may take place in a cell but to make it health-promoting requires concerted societal action.

As Louisa L. Williams observes, 'Fundamentally, our life is determined not by genetics but by epigenetics that is, the environment we live and create for ourselves primarily determines the expression of our genes and our level of health.'[7] As our scientific understanding of epigenetic mechanisms advances, we need to change social conditions that influence our gene expression. Some of these relate to personal behaviours but many are shared societal features. Even personal behaviours are influenced by social determinants. We need to alter the influences that drive epigenetic expression so that they can foster better health and not create disease. This requires collective action. We need to be connected, to create together the right conditions for health.

The Story of Stress

'I believe that stress is a factor in any bad health.'[1]

—Chris Shays

'Stress' is a word heard quite often in present times, as an explanation for both physical and mental disorders or even for sub-optimal performance in studies or work. Whether it is a student feeling stressed by academic and examination pressures, an employee responding to unrealistic deadlines imposed by the supervisor, a commuter stuck in stalled or slow-moving traffic or a soldier suffering from post-traumatic stress disorder (PTSD), stress has many negative connotations. It conjures up the image of a hurried, harried and harassed person who is in harm's way.

Why is stress such a bad word? How does it harm the body, mind and soul? Is stress always undesirable? How does one avoid it or learn to cope with it?

Hans Selye who coined the term 'stress' in 1936 defined it as 'the non-specific response of the body to any demand for change'.[2] This sounds innocuous but why has it become sinister in its implications, being blamed for heart attacks to stomach ulcers and high blood

34

pressure to diabetes? Stress is the collective term used to describe the sum total of the body's responses to a challenging situation. The challenge may be physical, mental or emotional. As long as the stimulus is sufficient to challenge you or even threaten you in any way, the evoked response adds up to 'stress'.

The 'Stress Response'

To understand the basis of the stress response, one has to go back to the days of our ancestors (the hunter–gatherers of early human history). When the caveman ventured into the forest to be confronted by the beast, the choice was 'fight or flight'. If he managed to hunt the prey, it would be his food. If the beast triumphed, the outcome of the encounter was the other way around. Even if the visit was intended merely to gather fruit, the threats around meant one had to be on guard or 'under stress'.

Under those circumstances, stress was an essential survival mechanism. The response to these challenges produced increased activity of the sympathetic nervous system and adrenal glands. Adrenaline and steroid hormones poured into the bloodstream on a command from the brain and orchestrated a whole series of military manoeuvres. Adrenaline raised the pulse rate and blood pressure so that more blood would flow to the exercising muscles.

The blood supply to the parts that were not actively engaged in combat or critical decisions was temporarily reduced. For example, blood supply was diverted from the stomach and intestines ('butterflies in the stomach' or 'stomach cramps') and the skin ('cold skin' or 'cold clammy hands'). The sweat glands were activated as the heat generated during muscular activity had to be quickly dissipated. The pupils dilated so that the gaze could take in the surroundings in a wide frame ('where is the beast coming from?').

The surge of adrenaline and steroids broke down glucose stores and raised blood glucose levels so that the brain (which had to make life-saving decisions in a split second) and the muscles (which had to help in fighting or fleeing) were well supplied with their fuel. Since exercising muscles offered greater resistance to blood flow, blood pressure rose to overcome that resistance and supply the muscles with adequate blood-bearing oxygen and glucose. Blood clotting tendency also increased to quickly seal off blood loss from any injury sustained during the fight or flight.

Why Is it a Problem Now?

Obviously, the stress response was very useful for human survival under conditions of adversity. When did it turn into an undesirable thing? It happened when we were catapulted into modernity, which brought about vastly different conditions of living. First, the nature of threats changed. They are more often than not, threats to our self-esteem or our tranquillity than to our physical survival. Second, the originally intended outlet of fight or flight does not usually operate in current times. You cannot flee from class to escape the assault on your self-esteem mounted by a teacher's unkind comments. Neither can an employee bash up the boss in retaliation for the hurt caused by harsh words or nasty behaviour.

Road rage too is rightly considered uncivilized behaviour. Anger mounts without physical release. So what happens is that the adrenaline and steroids do surge but the racing pulse, raised blood pressure, elevated blood sugar and thickening blood serve no 'useful' purpose as such. They only damage our bodies, like the engine of a stationary car gets overheated when the accelerator is pressed unnecessarily. The result is damage to blood vessels, heart attacks, paralytic strokes, diabetes and many more health hazards associated with modern living.

The problem is also that we suffer from chronic stress. While the acute stress response may have saved the lives of our ancestors, chronic stress due to repetitive daily threats (real and imaginary) wears our bodies down through a perpetual adrenaline whipping. Appetite is reduced and sleep is disturbed. The mind too is on the edge making us nervous, irritable, unable to concentrate and too ready to take offence.[3]

Is all stress bad? Not really. We do need some stress to help us perform better. If we do not see any challenges before us, we become inert and nonperforming. Some stress, therefore, is a positive stimulus and is creative. The batsman in cricket, who has a 'keen eye' as he takes his guard and the student, whose 'sharp mind' is ready to rapidly retrieve stored information as the question paper is being handed out, are responding to that positive stimulus that challenges their self-esteem but prods them to peak performance. An acute stress response can also be lifesaving in the face of danger. Would you keep very 'cool' and saunter nonchalantly across a busy road as vehicles come speeding at you?

On the other hand, excessive stress depletes reserves and leaves behind a drained body and distracted mind, which cannot respond to challenges adequately. This is just like a musical instrument with strings. If the strings are too lax, you cannot produce good music. If they are too taut, they do not resonate well either. You need just the right amount of tension in the wire to produce the best result. The right quantum of stress represents the 'careful' that is poised between 'careless' and 'careworn'.

How to Reduce Stress?

So how does one avoid or cope with stress so that it does not become excessive? First, we should stop misreading minor problems as major threats. Such misperceptions needlessly trigger the stress response. Reasoning with a calm mind will help us recognize that many things that seem to upset us are not really threats to our physical well-being or mental self-esteem. Some people use religion and belief in God to filter these perceived threats before they evoke the stress response ('God is there to take care—why should I worry?'). Others use meditation as a shield to deflect these arrows from striking the mind.

Even without these aids, we can train our minds not to recognize or register unpleasant events as threats. With a strong sense of self-esteem, we do not feel easily vulnerable. If a person is confident, many irritants will be brushed away by the mind and will not register on the 'threatometer'. As former Australian cricket captain Steve Waugh said, if you 'learn to back yourself', you can cope with a lot of pressure.

Music, enjoyable reading, the company of friends or family and affectionate pets are among helpful diversions that distract our minds from the sources of stress and dilute its effects. Sometimes, it helps to talk over things with a close friend who may help you see things in a different light and remove misperceptions of a threat. Social support systems make you more confident of 'survival' and reassure you that help is available to overcome challenges.[4]

It also helps to be better prepared for events that may prove stressful. Such preparation boosts your confidence and you do not feel threatened since you know that the challenge can be met. Whether it is study or sport, job or juggling, the secret of success is awareness, anticipation and adequate preparation in a planned manner. Being ready keeps your stress down to the right level.

Physical activity and exercise help too. Exercise evokes acute stress-like responses with respect to pulse rate, blood pressure and many other components of the stress response.[5] However, repetitive exercise conditions the body to accept more and more challenges with less and less adrenaline rise. Gradually the body gets used to performing a lot of work at lower heart rates and blood pressure, with higher reserves left to meet further challenges. Exercise breeds cross-tolerance to mental stress. Those who are physically active have a less intense adrenaline response to mental or emotional challenges and cope better with stressful situations. Indeed, the original outlet for the stress response was physical activity (when our forefathers ran after or away from the beast). What better way to release our stress than to spiritedly chase a tennis ball or skilfully evade the pursuit of your soccer opponent! Perhaps office employees too could persuade their boss to install a table-tennis table in the office. Happy hunting and safe gathering in sport instead of a dangerous forest!

Physical activity has been found to be beneficial for arterial blood pressure in school children.[6] One of the ways by which this happens is through better cross-tolerance to mental stress. When children are challenged with stressful situations, such as complex mathematical problems, their blood pressure usually rises. However, children who are physically active through regular games and sports have a much lower rise in blood pressure than children who are usually sedentary. Physical activity promotes not only fitness but also cross-tolerance to stress. It can be great fun too!

Not eating regularly also creates a stress-like situation in the body. If we skip breakfast while going to school or work, the blood sugar levels are low. So the body pumps in stress hormones to raise them just in case we get into trouble. When you do meet a stressful situation in school or work, the adrenaline levels that are already high rise even higher and the stress response goes into overdrive. A proper meal keeps the stress hormones at a low level, and they will rise only when really needed and even then be at moderate levels. Have you noticed that you are likelier to pick up fights when you are hungry? We now even have a term coined for this—'hangry'![7]

Connection to Others and Environment

John Hunter was a celebrated surgeon and anatomist of the eighteenth century who worked at St. George's Hospital in London. He was also the first to clearly describe the symptoms of cardiac angina based on his own experience of chest pain. Known to be easily provoked, he is said to have perceptively remarked, '*my life* is at the mercy of the scoundrel who *chooses* to put *me* in a passion'.[8] True to that prediction, he suffered a fatal heart attack during a heated argument over admission of medical students in a stormy hospital board meeting.

While stress is a phenomenon experienced by our bodies, it is related to how we react to others around us, the events in our lives and the physical and social environments in which we live and function. Being stuck in noisy traffic can grate on our nerves while poverty, stigma, discrimination, inequality and injustice can make daily life a terrible tale of unrelieved stress. Conflict in society, bad politics and lack of empathy in human relations can create stressful conditions that can endanger the health of many.

Unless we are monks and nuns in solitary retreat, our social relationships will reflect on how protected we can be from harmful stress in our daily lives. So, our connections do matter! Together, we can create social and environmental conditions that do not threaten our physical safety and mental tranquillity. We can avail the benefits of creative stress while avoiding the harmful effects of corrosive stress.

Migration Mash-up:
Gene–Environmental Interactions

'Migrants and refugees are not pawns on the chessboard
of humanity.'[1]

—POPE FRANCIS

Extensive interactions between genes and environment are brought out vividly when we study the health of people who moved out of the country or region where they were born to another country or region that has different geographic, environmental and sociocultural features. Sometimes it might take years of acculturation to manifest distinctive biological effects. The time for transition is determined by how malleable migrant behaviours are.

Why Do People Migrate?

Migration is prompted by different forces. It may be voluntary migration or forced migration. People may be choosing to migrate because they seek better educational or employment opportunities. They may be forced to migrate because of adverse climatic changes,

41

extreme weather events, war, conflict or persecution. An extreme form of forced migration was the slave trade, which in modern days is mirrored by human trafficking

When migration involves people voluntarily moving to new places for education or employment, especially to other countries, they are usually in better health than their peers in their home country. They have to be fit enough to travel and often need to produce evidence of good health status by the countries to which they wish to emigrate. They may have health challenges when they initially face days of struggle in the new country. However, they need to have the stamina to weather those challenges and advance in life. This was the experience of most migrants in the nineteenth and twentieth centuries.

However, the twenty-first century has seen higher levels of forced migration.[2] The journey to new lands is undertaken in perilous conditions, with lives lost on the way. The arrival of the migrants is often unwelcome to the existing inhabitants and they are frequently subjected to xenophobia, segregation, discrimination and even violence. This has an adverse effect on their health. Even if they are accepted grudgingly, the absence of assured health and social services poses risks to their physical and mental well-being.

Within-country migration provides a mixed pattern of motives and vulnerabilities. Those who are from wealthy or income secure families are usually in good health and advance further in health gains as they climb up the income and social ladders offered by migration.[3] Those who are in low paid, often dangerous occupations are subjected to hardships and assured of neither good health nor affordable healthcare.

Migration, however, offers many opportunities for studying the manner in which the health of the migrants is affected by their new environment. This is mediated by changes in ambient temperature, water and sanitation systems, pollution levels, changing dietary preferences and composition, availability and safety of transport systems, level of physical activity required or enabled, uptake or giving up of addictive behaviours and entry into new social networks. Many of these shape the way people behave in the new environment and expose their bodies to new influences.

The genes they carry had been coded to the earlier environment and their expression can be altered by the new environment. The induced epigenetic changes may stretch across several generations. The microbiome too is altered due to new dietary and environmental influences. This changes the risk of several diseases. We see the evidence of both mismatch and adaptation in the health experiences of migrants.

Migrant Variations in Disease Risk

Several theories have been proposed to explain differences in disease risk that have been observed in migrant population groups when compared to populations in their countries of origin, populations that are 'local' to the host countries and migrant groups who originated from other countries but now share the same living environment in their common host country. Three different theories that are discussed in this regard are the 'Thrifty Gene Hypothesis', the 'Thrifty Phenotype Hypothesis' and the 'Drifty Genotype Hypothesis'. While the genetic component features prominently in these titles, the originating ancestral living environment or recent pre-natal and early childhood environments of nurture are important determinants of genetic selection and gene expression.

James V. Neel proposed the 'Thrifty Gene' in 1962,[4] questioning whether it was 'rendered detrimental by progress'. He suggested that when populations lived with fluctuations in food availability, selection pressures favoured the perpetuation of genetic alleles that helped to conserve energy and reduce its consumption. Thus insulin-resistant muscles would not burn up more energy, permitting the brain to use the blood glucose for survival. High levels of physical activity would reduce insulin resistance, if that too was a survival requirement.

In societies with more assured abundance of food and less physical activity, this 'thrifty gene' would be counterproductive and lead to higher incidence of diabetes in populations that have preserved the thrifty gene. Similarly, the preferential selection of salt-sensitive alleles would have helped in climes and times where the body needed to optimally utilize limited salt availability in hot and humid climates. However, urbanization, industrialization and globalization of trade has made salt available everywhere on store shelves and the explosive growth of marketing in salt-loaded ultra-processed foods has increased salt consumption far beyond physiologic requirements. This has created a mismatch between salt-handling genetic mechanisms crafted in different conditions and contemporary dietary patterns.

While the thrifty gene is an attractive and plausible proposition, it does not explain some of the maladapted responses that have emerged in relatively recent history. Coronary heart disease in South Asians has come to the fore over the past 70 years. Diabetes has been noted among the Indian rich for a longer period but the huge epidemic that has engulfed many sections of the population is a relatively recent occurrence of less than a century.

This is true of many other populations like the aboriginal and indigenous populations in North America, Australasia and the Pacific Islands who have been caught in the grip of commercial marketing of food products and beverages with high levels of sugar, salt and unhealthy fats. Many of these groups have had an experience of undernutrition and poverty imposed by recent colonial history. Researchers have also contested the theories of ancient and prolonged famines that were proposed to advance the selection and propagation of the thrifty gene. So, other explanations were sought.

The explanation came in the form of the thrifty phenotype. If the foetus in the womb is undernourished, because the mother herself has been poorly fed as a child and/or has poor nutrient intake during the pregnancy, the growing baby is epigenetically programmed to express the genes in a manner that prioritizes survival. Conserving nutrients for the brain and nervous system becomes a high priority. Fat is stored in the abdomen as an energy reserve, at the expense of the muscle mass. Insulin resistance is helpful in providing a steady supply of glucose to the brain while the muscles are not permitted easy access for quick utilization as their fuel. All of these adaptive measures do not go back several generations and centuries, but can happen as an intergenerational effect in a single pregnancy. Evidence in support of the thrifty phenotype, proposed first by Barker, has found support from studies across several populations in the world. Some of the epigenetic effects can carry across generations if gene expression is not markedly reset by fresh environmental influences.

A variation on these themes, but less commonly cited, involves the drifty gene. It has been argued by J. R. Speakman[5] that the modern distribution of obese phenotypes arises from a 'genetic drift' in the genes encoding the regulatory system that places an upper limit on our body fatness. It has been proposed that the genetic drift started in our ancestors when they escaped from constant predatory threat. You cannot run fast from the predators if you are fat but once the predators are overcome with fire to scare them, weapons to kill them and chariots to speed away, the genes can drift away from the limits on obesity. While interesting, this hypothesis too has its origins in the experiences of ancient populations, like the thrifty gene hypothesis. The relatively recent nature of the global obesity epidemic is not explained by the theory.

Both the thrifty gene and drifty gene hypotheses depend on genetic changes occurring at the population level in our ancients, either through selection or drift. They developed during periods when food systems did not have an overabundance of supply, most people were physically active and stress levels were not pegged at high levels throughout the day. The thrifty phenotype, in contrast, emerges at the individual level, due to adverse nutritional and stress environments during pregnancy and early childhood. While it is a determinant at the individual level, it can manifest in many persons who share the same developmental experience in underprivileged sections of an inequitable society. So, it can be reflected at the population level.

The thrifty phenotype[6] can explain the relatively recent surge in obesity, cardiovascular disease and diabetes the world over. The trigger, however, remains an environment that is replete with an abundance of unhealthy foods, low in physical activity and high in repetitive or prolonged stressful events. While all the three theories remain as contestants in the debating arena of why diseases of maladapted modernity are rapidly rising, the thrifty phenotype appears to be the presently favoured one, with the backing of epigenetic data.

Over the last forty years, several studies have emerged to assess the risk of cardiovascular disease and diabetes in migrant populations, in comparison to long-term resident local populations.[7, 8] These have provided valuable insights into evolving disease patterns among migrants, as a result of gene–environment interactions. Such studies have involved migrants from the African continent, Caribbean countries, Indian sub-continent, South East Asia, Japan and China. They have studied first- and second-generation migrants and included diverse socio-economic groups.

African-origin Migrants

In the early 1980s, a study from Kenya compared blood pressure levels in subsistence farmers of the Luo tribe who lived in a rural environment with the tribesmen who had moved to the urban setting of Nairobi.[9] It was observed that blood pressure did not rise with age among the rural adults. However, those who migrated had higher blood pressure levels, with an age-related rise clearly evident. Higher dietary salt intake, lower dietary potassium intake and higher sodium to potassium ratios in the urine characterized the urban migrants. The rise in the level of blood pressure in the urban migrants positively correlated with the length of their stay in Nairobi.

High levels of hypertension and diabetes have also been noted in persons of African ethnicity who migrated to the USA and some European countries. African Americans in the USA have 1.3 and 1.6 times higher prevalence of adult onset diabetes (Type 2) and hypertension respectively, when compared with Americans of European ancestry.[10]

Those with African ancestry have been shown to be more resistant to the effect of insulin on various body tissues. Adult-onset diabetes is characterized by resistance of cell membranes to the action of insulin. Higher prevalence of Type 2 diabetes was noted in persons of African ancestry living in Netherlands, when compared to persons of similar ancestry living in the United Kingdom. Even for persons of European ancestry, diabetes prevalence was higher among the European Dutch when compared to the European English. This suggests that the living environment is important in determining the manner and level to which ethnic susceptibility expresses itself.

Higher salt sensitivity, of blood pressure response to salt consumption, has been observed among persons of African ancestry who have been studied in different countries. It has been hypothesized that such heightened sensitivity to salt intake has developed as an adaptive response to hot climatic conditions in the African continent. Such sensitivity may have been especially needed in the past for those living away from the coast with limited availability of salt.

When people from Africa's hinterland were captured and cruelly transported to other countries, especially to America, they carried their salt sensitivity with them. Genetic selection for salt sensitivity would have been advantageous for Africans living in their home continent in the Middle Ages. However, it would prove counterproductive in different geographies and in modern times when dietary salt intake rose markedly due to the nature of foods consumed and the climate no longer demanded the protective effect of salt sensitivity. This is the basis for the 'thrifty gene hypothesis'.

Japanese Migrants

A large number of Japanese people migrated to Hawaii and California in the late nineteenth and early twentieth centuries. Starting from the early 1960s, researchers examined the pattern of diseases among men of Japanese ethnicity in Japan (Nippon), Hawaii (Honolulu) and California (San Francisco). This was labelled the Ni-Hon-San study.[11]

The study revealed that the risk of brain stroke (cerebrovascular disease), which was very high among the Japanese in Japan, declined progressively as they settled in Honolulu and San Francisco. The Japanese in their home country had a high incidence of bleeding or haemorrhagic strokes. However, they acquired a new vascular factor that was more prevalent in their new environments—high blood cholesterol associated with fat-rich diets. With rising blood cholesterol levels associated with their westward migration, the risk of coronary heart disease spiralled up as they moved to Honolulu and San Francisco.

In their home country, the Japanese continued to have very low levels of coronary heart disease, even as they aged. Alterations in diet and social milieu seemed to result in changes in body weight and blood cholesterol levels, with accompanying changes in disease patterns. Over time, the migrants exhibited disease patterns intermediate between the land of origin and the land of migration, with higher coronary risk than the Japanese back home but lower risk than noted in white Americans.

That is true of most first- and second-generation migrant populations. However, neither of those populations are static as changes in socio-economic development, culture and adaptation to new scientific knowledge change disease risks and profile at both points of migration over time. The host population too undergo changes in their behaviours and the migrants adapt to that cultural churn, with the disease risk getting further modified.

South Asian Migrants

The experience of South Asian migrants has been somewhat dissimilar. Since the 1950s, it has been observed that migrants of South Asian origin (mainly from India, Pakistan, Bangladesh and Sri Lanka) exhibited a much higher risk of coronary heart disease, compared to local populations and other migrant groups, across many countries.[12]

This risk was certainly much higher than persons of similar age and gender in the country of origin but, contrary to the Japanese experience, higher than observed even in the local ethnic groups of the countries to which they had migrated. This extra risk was being manifested across several countries and several generations. Initially, the high risk was noted through inter-ethnic comparisons in Malaya and Uganda and later through similar comparisons in the UK, Singapore, the USA, Canada, Mauritius and South Africa.

Apart from early onset and extensive coronary disease, a distinctive risk profile emerged in South Asian migrants. There was a high incidence of diabetes or pre-diabetes, associated with high levels of atherogenic triglyceride lipids and low levels of protective HDL-cholesterol in the blood. While general obesity levels were unremarkable, there was a prominent pattern of fat deposition in the abdomen, with the protuberant belly becoming a striking visual hallmark.

Subsequent studies in India showed this pattern among urban Indians.[13] A study[14] of factory workers in urban India showed that those who migrated to urban areas quickly acquired the urban risk profile, compared to their siblings who stayed behind in rural areas. Abdominal girth, body weight, blood pressure, blood sugar, blood fats and insulin levels all went up to higher risk levels within five years of migration. Other studies comparing Punjabis and Gujaratis in India to Punjabi and Gujarati migrants in the UK also revealed an increased risk of diabetes and heart disease associated with international migration.[15]

In contrast to the experience of Japanese migrants in the Ni-Hon-San study, the risk among Indian and other South Asian migrants to other countries was not intermediate between the risk levels of home and adopted countries. The risk of cardiovascular and metabolic disorders was higher than that seen in both home and the adopted countries. Acculturation alone did not account for the markedly increased risk among the migrants. This suggests that there is a genetic or epigenetically programmed susceptibility that is expressed very little in the rural Indian environment, but expressed with rising severity in the urban Indian environment and much more aggressively in the global migrant environments.

What is the likely explanation for this phenomenon? The 'thrifty gene' hypothesis was invoked but there is no historical basis to believe that Indians were starving in pre-colonial times. Quite the contrary, economists report that India contributed a quarter of the global economy in the Middle Ages. A 'thrifty phenotype' that emerged in the late twentieth century offers a better explanation.

Intra-uterine and early childhood undernutrition condition the foetus in the womb and the very young child to conserve energy as body fat rather than as lean muscle that quickly burns up calories. Abdominal fat offers the best deposit and provides survival advantage to the endangered baby. As the child grows, there is a mismatch between this metabolic programming and energy intake, with preferential storage as body fat that has serious health consequences in terms of cardiovascular disease and diabetes.

This programming effect can carry over a few generations due to the transmission of epigenetic modifications. So, when an Indian migrant moves to a calorie-rich environment, the embers of programmed susceptibility are stoked by altered diets and lowered by physical activity. Inflammation is triggered, leading to cardiovascular disease and diabetes.

The Environment Matters!

Whatever be the mechanism involved, it is clear that the environment determines the way genes are selected for survival due to evolutionary pressures created by the living conditions or genes are modified in their expression through epigenetic changes induced by the environment. We are in a position to influence these by our choices in how societies should live. There is no reason why a Japanese person moving to the USA or an Indian moving to the UK should acquire a higher risk of getting a heart attack if dietary patterns remain healthy, physical activity is built into daily routine and stress does not constantly grate on the mind and the blood vessels.

Migration to a new environment creates natural experiments that give us insights into gene–environmental interactions. Why do Indian immigrants to the UK acquire a higher coronary risk than Indians in the home country and also more than Afro-Caribbean immigrants to the UK? Why do the latter have a lower coronary risk than Indian immigrants and British citizens of European descent but have a higher risk of hypertension and kidney disease than either of them?

It appears that when the same gene pool operates in different environments (for example, Indians in India and Indians in the UK), the risk factors like changed diets, physical activity patterns and adaptation-related stress levels play a major role. When different immigrant groups are compared in the same environment of the adopted country, influences of the different gene pools, which were selectively propagated in the environments of their home countries, will become more prominent.

Cultural differences, such as dietary preferences, cooking methods and social interactions, too play a role in differentiating the risks to the varied immigrant groups. Over time, especially in the second- and third-generation immigrants, the cultural and dietary differences between the long-term 'local' ethnic groups and the immigrants blur and epigenetic influences too may become less prominent. However, the interplay between the genetic influences and the environment is the background against which still discernible ethnic differences in risk will play out.

Migration will entail change, but the change should be for the better, not worse. Blending the best of different cultures will add to the healthy life years of migrants. Genes provide the paint but the picture we create with them, on the canvas of our living environment, is dependent on our choices and talent. Creating that environment requires a collective societal effort. We are connected to our ancestors, our contemporaries and to the future generations, through the genes that we inherit and pass on and the environments we create to influence gene selection and expression.

PART II

Nutrition

'Good nutrition will prevent 95 per cent of all disease.'[*]

—LINUS PAULING

---

* Details available at http://www.justaddgoodstuff.com/2013/06/13/good-nutrition-will-prevent-95-per-cent-of-all-diseases/

Selective Nutrients to Composite Diets

'Good nutrition creates health in all areas of our existence.
All parts are interconnected.'[1]

—T. COLLIN CAMPBELL

Diet is the food we consume and nutrition is what it provides in terms of nourishment to the body. Nutrition is clearly fundamental to health, wellness and longevity. This is conventional wisdom that everyone acquires as they grow up and are reminded of by parents and teachers. If anyone has not already registered the message, media features and industry advertising saturate us with messaging on what to eat and what to avoid to stay healthy or grow healthier. Everyone espouses the vital role of good nutrition at every stage of life.

It is nutrition that builds our body, whether it is blood, bone, brain or muscle. It helps in making hormones and building immunity. It enables reproduction. When nutrition goes awry, inflammatory processes can get activated to damage many parts of our body, increase the clotting tendency in the blood or block blood vessels to cut off the supply to the heart or brain. An unbalanced diet leads

55

to general or abdominal obesity, both of which are associated with increased inflammation, heart disease, diabetes and risk of cancer. Nutrition is not just the fuel that gives us the energy to lead our daily lives. It creates and nurtures the very fabric of our existence, the whole human body.

It is a big challenge to understand how we can acquire good health through our daily diets. This is where consensus breaks down, within the scientific community, the food industry, popular belief and media messaging. This results in confusion and contradictions, which leaves the common person bewildered most of the time and often cynical about dietary advice. It does not help that serious scientific positions as well as media enthusiasm for fad diets change frequently.

Much of the confusion arises from a reductionist approach to scientific enquiry. There is a widely prevalent credo among researchers that attribution of benefit or harm is possible only when individual nutrients are studied in isolation or specific food items are assessed. This is usually done through long-term follow-up of some population groups or through randomized controlled trials of dietary interventions. Comparison of different populations helps in identifying why certain diets may be healthier than others but such ecological comparisons are vulnerable to confounding or distortions by many other factors that may be operating at the population level. So, such studies are thought to be hypothesis generating rather than hypothesis testing.

A Reductionist View of Specific Nutrients

Nutrition scientists were happiest to begin by pursuing a reductionist approach, breaking down diets to the molecular level. Not just the effect of carbohydrates, fats and fats as a class but the specific effect of every nutrient in each class. Of course, it is good to know that from the point of view of understanding the physiological effects of each nutrient. However, such knowledge is not always helpful in predicting how the body behaves when that nutrient is added, enhanced, reduced or eliminated from the diet. So also with individual food items.

That is because diets are composed of many food items, each with many nutrients. They balance, supplement, enhance, diminish or counteract each other's effects on the different body systems. A reductionist approach to the study of isolated nutrients or single food items does not provide adequate evidence of how the human body responds to them when they are consumed with other nutrients or food items.

To understand this, let us look at the popular discussion of the value of antioxidants on human health.[2] These are nutrients like Vitamin E, beta-carotene and Vitamin C. Long-term follow-up studies of population cohorts suggested that foods containing these antioxidants were protective against heart disease, cancer and some other disorders associated with high oxidative stress. The industry decided to market individual antioxidants or combinations thereof with gusto, packing them in pills and pouches instead of natural foods.

Other scientists set out to evaluate the protective effects of individual antioxidants on disease outcomes through randomized controlled clinical trials that are less susceptible to methodological bias than cohort studies. In most cases, the antioxidant supplements conferred no benefit. In some cases, they actually caused harm. So, does this debunk the protective value of antioxidant vitamins?

There can be several explanations for these contradictions. The observational cohort studies may indeed have been biased. The doses administered may have been inappropriate. The pills taken at one meal may not have retained the blood levels to counter the oxidative stress related to other meals. The synthetic chemicals in the pills may have been different isomers of natural vitamins, with less effect.

More likely, the many phytonutrients in fruit and vegetables, the natural sources of these anti-oxidants, would have had potentiating interactions that the isolated synthetic vitamins would not have. Natural fruit and vegetables are power packed with hundreds of phytonutrients like vitamins, minerals, flavonoids and fibre, which act in concert.[3] They contain potassium that balances the effect of dietary sodium, lowers raised blood pressure and reduces the risk of strokes. The protective role of fruit and vegetables against heart disease and cancer has been corroborated by several later cohort studies and clinical trials too. Reductionism lost that round. Score one for Nature!

Similar debates continue to be waged around food items like fish. The problem arises when fish oils are put into a capsule for conducting trials. The differential effects of the two main fish oils (eicosa pentaenoicacid or EPA and docosa hexaenoic acid or DHA) together modulate the biological effects in the body but clinical trials that use different ratios of these come up with different results when evaluating the impact on vascular events or heart rhythm abnormalities.[4] Yet again, the capsule is a distraction from the nutritious value of the natural fish diet. Also, extrapolating from the composition of a single food item its physiological effects on the body, based on a single nutrient in its composition, has proved inaccurate and even counterproductive as in the case of nuts and eggs.

The single food item issue has been a problem in many other cases too. Take butter versus margarine. For several years butter was banished because of saturated fat content and margarine was feted. However, the finding that trans-fats in margarine were far more dangerous than the saturated fat in butter dethroned the pretender. The manner in which the food item is prepared or consumed is also not often taken into account in research studies. Was the meat smoked or salted? Did the fruit lose its fibre and liberate free sugars in its extracted juice? Were the vegetables sautéed, fried or boiled till the nutrients leeched out?

Composite Diets

Such contradictions and controversies, which abound in reductionist research on individual nutrients and solitary food items, have led to researchers asking whether it is the total composition of the diet, which is far more predictive of health outcomes. The interest was stoked by evidence of longevity and good health conferred by the Mediterranean diet and the Okinawa diet as well as the composite DASH diet, which was trialled for treatment of hypertensions.[5]

A major finding of studies conducted on several of the composite diets is that the dietary pattern is what is beneficial and not any individual component. This has been clearly demonstrated in studies of the Mediterranean diet that struggled to find a single component (such as olive oil) to which the protective effect could be attributed.[6] However, as the score increased of the nine identified components of the Mediterranean diet, the protective effect rose! This is what scientists call a 'dose–response' relationship. What this finding demonstrates is that a reductionist lens fails to detect the health benefits of a composite diet.

It is not necessary that the whole world should adopt the Mediterranean diet. Local cuisines can adopt the principles of a healthy composite diet, combining easily accessible and relatively inexpensive ingredients. Harvard researchers[7] assessed the health outcomes of a 'prudent' diet and a 'western diet'. The former is characterized by higher intake of fruits, vegetables, legumes, whole grains and fish. The latter consists of red and processed meats, refined grains, sweets and desserts. Ultra-processed foods dominate harmful diets, while natural foods are plentiful in a prudent diet. These principles can be used to promote prudent diets appropriate to each cultural, climatic and economic context.

Guiding Principles

The key guiding principles of a healthy dietary habit are like the four legs of the dining table. They are variety, balance, moderation and regularity. These are the legs on which a health promoting diet will need to stand. Dietary diversity is key to good nutrition and provides balance, while enhancing enjoyment. A prudent diet, created and consumed based on these principles, will help to make and maintain good health over the life course.

Predominantly plant-based diets are best suited for human health as well as ecological sustainability. As we move from the reductionist paradigm of looking at nutrients in isolation, we can also embrace the holistic vision of creating food systems that can protect the planet that gifts us life sustaining nutrition.

The Many Faces of Malnutrition

'Malnutrition can be as common in poverty as in wealth, one for the lack of food, the other for the lack of knowledge of food.'[1]

—T.K. Naliaka

If all of humanity was fair and sensible, no one would fall ill from lack of nutritious food or become obese by consuming unhealthy foods. However, we see these pictures of poor nutrition still widespread in this century where scientific advancements in knowledge and technology should have freed us from these problems. Undernutrition continues to exist in many parts of the world, while being overweight and obesity are a rapidly expanding form of global malnutrition. Along with the 'hidden hunger' of micronutrient deficiencies, where the physique may appear healthily nourished but is deficient in vital nutrients like some vitamins and minerals, these constitute the three faces of malnutrition.

While undernutrition and malnutrition have been popularly used synonymously, and the term 'overnutrition' has been in vogue for describing being overweight and obesity, they are terms carried over from times when the world of human nutrition focused mainly on adequacy of total calorie intake (energy) and not on nutrient quality. Indeed, micronutrient deficiencies are a form of undernutrition too. Overweight and obese persons may have higher body weights and body fat than what is considered healthy, but they too may be deficient in both desirable macro and micronutrients. Their diets are often low in consumption of healthy foods like fibre and nutrient rich fruit and vegetables and have inadequate levels of micronutrients. So, it is a case of inappropriate nutrition rather than overnutrition.

Therefore, the full spectrum of malnutrition should include undernutrition, overweight-obesity and micronutrient deficiencies. To argue against simplistic classifications, we also need to remind ourselves that malnourished persons who are underweight or stunted also have disproportionately high levels of body fat and less muscle mass, thereby overlapping metabolically with those who are overweight or obese.

Manifestations of Undernutrition

Undernutrition manifests in children as stunting, wasting or being underweight. Stunting is when the child is short for their age (measured as height for age).[2] It represents a state of chronic or long-term malnourishment that began in pregnancy or very early childhood. Later feeding focusing only on energy (calorie) compensation, without attention to diet quality, often leads to obesity rather than a catch-up spurt in height.

A better approach would be to provide a balanced nutrient and fibre-rich food rather than just focus on calories. Wasting is when the child is too thin for the level of their height (weight for height).[3] Underweight is when the child is lower in weight than appropriate for their age (weight for age).[4] In all of these cases, a nutritionally balanced diet is needed rather a narrow focus on calories.

Undernutrition carries a huge penalty for growth and development. In childhood, survival is threatened by susceptibility to infections. Compromised physical growth makes the child forego the benefits of a physically active childhood. There is a loss of brain power as cognitive function is impaired and educational attainment suffers, with later consequences for employment, income and consequently for health. Anaemia in childhood has consequences for activity and learning ability. In women of reproductive age, anaemia can compromise the health and lives of mothers and their babies. Micronutrient deficiencies can cause a variety of disorders from hypothyroidism to lowered immunity.

Undernutrition during the foetal period or early childhood leads to epigenetic changes or metabolic programming that is linked to increased risk of hypertension, heart disease, diabetes and several other chronic diseases in adulthood.[5] In the elderly, malnutrition makes them easy prey to infections and dementia. However measured, malnutrition is a curse to human health across the life course.

Overweight and Obesity

Overweight and obesity too have undergone definitional debates, on the criteria and cut-offs to be applied. Body mass index (BMI), a ratio of weight and height, is the conventional index for judging if a person is underweight, normal weight, overweight or obese. It is expressed as weight in kilograms divided by a squared measure of height in metres. A BMI of less than 18 is labelled as underweight, between 18 to 25 as normal body weight, from 25 to 30 as overweight and over 30 as obese. These are by western standards but are still widely used for international comparisons. Being overweight and obesity are associated with increasing levels of health risk due to diabetes, heart attacks, stroke, cancer and many other diseases.

BMI, when used as an indicator of excess weight, is usually interpreted to be due to excess body fat (adipose tissue). It need not always be so, as a very muscular athlete can have a high BMI without high body adiposity. Even persons with high bone weight may be labelled as overweight without having a high level of body fat. However, this has become the most commonly used measure for characterizing being overweight and obesity in individuals and populations and a surrogate for undesirable levels of body fat.

By relying solely on BMI cut-offs, the problem of underestimating the risk associated with high body fat appears to be high in some populations. Persons of Asian ethnicity, especially South Asians, have higher levels of body fat and associated metabolic risk at BMI levels lower than in western populations. Recognizing this, WHO recommended lower public health and clinical thresholds for assessment of risk in Asians—BMI of 23 for overweight and 27.5 for obesity.

Distribution of Body Fat

The debate does not end there. The distribution of fat in the human body matters, even more than the total fat or BMI. If the fat is located more within the abdomen, around the organs rather than the abdominal wall, it carries greater danger. This visceral fat is associated with high levels of inflammation in the body and also with a wide range of metabolic abnormalities in the composition and levels of blood fats, glucose and clotting mediators.

About a third of the persons with diabetes in India have been reported to be thin with central rather than general obesity.[6] Early onset of hypertension, diabetes and heart disease in adulthood is a feature in India and other countries of South Asia. While no genetic marker of high predictive value has been found, patterns of imbalanced nutrition, commencing from childhood or acquired in adulthood, are likely to be responsible.

Abdominal or central obesity has been conventionally measured by the ratio of the circumference of the waist to that of the hip. A high waist to hip ratio is usually associated with a male pattern of obesity ('apple' shape), while more fat around the hips is usually associated with a female pattern of obesity ('pear' shape). The former is metabolically dangerous and associated with a wide variety of inflammatory and chronic degenerative diseases. The latter form is safer as it is not associated with the same type of metabolic abnormalities or level of inflammatory responses in the body.

Even with the waist circumference alone or with the waist to hip ratio, lower cut-offs were recommended for Asians, especially Indians, for a better prediction of the risk of cardiovascular disease and diabetes, than those applied to western populations. Since hip measurement is often difficult to measure, waist to height ratio has also emerged as a suitable measure of abdominal obesity. A waist to height ratio of over 0.5 in older children, adolescents and adults provides a reasonable clue to the presence of central or abdominal obesity.[7]

Ideally, both general obesity and abdominal obesity should be avoided. Both are associated with a variety of health disorders. Imbalance of nutrients, along with inadequate physical activity lead to either or both of these conditions. Metabolic abnormalities and inflammatory damage to many organs are noted in both, more so with abdominal (visceral) obesity.

A balanced diet, adequate but not excess in calories and high in plant products but restricted in sugar, salt and unhealthy fats, helps to reduce the body fat content. Regular aerobic physical activity and resistance exercises will help build lean muscle mass and reduce the body fat content.

'Hidden Hunger'

While we mostly think of major categories of nutrients like carbohydrates, fats and proteins in our food, there are many nutrients that are present in small quantities but are vital for our health. These are vitamins and minerals. Their deficiencies, labelled as 'hidden hunger' can cause severe disease.[8]

Diets deficient in iron, folic acid or vitamin B12 can cause anaemia. Women and children in many parts of the world suffer from anaemia, which reduces their functional ability. Deficiency of iodine results in reduced function of the thyroid gland. Reduced production of thyroid hormones can lead to cretinism and retardation of physical and mental growth in children.

Vitamin A deficiency can lead to blindness. Zinc deficiency leads to impaired immunity and growth and affects the functioning of several body systems. Vitamin D deficiency leads to rickets and poor skeletal growth in children. It too impairs immunity. Other vitamins, such as Vitamin C, too serve important functions in human physiology, maintain tissue integrity and help in preventing diseases.

Deficiencies result from a variety of reasons, from the nature of crops to types of diet. Micronutrient deficiencies frequently accompany undernutrition. Even diets high in calories can be deficient in micronutrients if the types of foods consumed have low levels of these. So, this category of nutritional deficiency can also overlap with being overweight and obesity.

Eliminating Malnutrition

All three forms of malnutrition are related to our dietary patterns. They are in turn determined by our food systems; they determine the availability and affordability of food, trade and commerce, which influence distribution and marketing, economic and social factors that determine the individual's dietary practices. Food processing affects dietary quality, while food fortification attempts to replenish missing micronutrients. Climate change, by imposing heat and water stresses on crops, can deplete both the quantity and the quality of nutrients available to all human beings.

All forms of malnutrition represent failure of human society to develop and sustain the required level and diversity of food production that can provide the right level of health promoting diets for every human being. Malnutrition does not occur purely by individual choice. It is the product of economic, social, commercial and climatic factors that steer the functioning of our society. These can be changed, if human beings act to change those determinants to align them better with the nutrition and health goals of the whole global population.

For that, we need to give up self-centred behaviours and think together as a social collective. If we think of how much healthcare costs can be saved by preventing nutrition-related diseases and how much of brain power and productivity can be protected and promoted by preventing undernutrition in children and anaemia in women, there is a compelling case for global solidarity in seeking nutrition security for all human beings. Apart, of course, from the moral imperative. To achieve that solidarity, we need to connect as humans—for advancing our collective action on the many interwoven connected determinants of healthy nutrition.

Agriculture, Food Systems
and Health

'We urgently need to do things differently and act
holistically to transform our agri-food systems. Because
soon, the table will need to be set for 10 billion people!'[1]

—QU DONGYU

Unless you are a hermit living in splendid seclusion in a forest
(in which case you would not be reading this book), you need
some other human beings working somewhere in this wide world
to give you the food that you consume daily. Even if you cook it
yourself, the ingredients have come from other human hands that
grew, gathered, processed, packed, stored, sold and delivered them
to you.

Even the hermit would need to depend on the many other life
forms in the forest, especially plants, to obtain the food needed
for the body's sustenance. Also, what would the hermit do if the
forest is getting destroyed by loggers or by wild fires sparked by
climate change? So, humans are dependent for their daily nutrition

needs on their connections to complex food systems, whether they are created by nature or crafted by humans. Indeed, even the food systems that are designed by humans originate in nature, though they may perversely end up destroying nature.

What are Food Systems?

Food systems involve the production, preservation, storage, transport, processing, trade, distribution, packaging, promotion, pricing and retail sale of food products—commencing from their natural or synthetic origins and ending with the delivery to the person who consumes them. The quantity, quality, safety and affordability of the foods we consume are determined by the food systems. The way they operate can make or mar human health.

Apart from the complexity that food systems have within themselves, they also interact with the larger ecosystem comprising land, water and climate, they impact the levels of energy utilization— be it for agriculture of diverse crops or the manufacture of myriad products. These interactions impact human health through pathways that involve nutrition, climate change, water security, chemical pollution and zoonotic pathogen transmission.

The twentieth century saw the industrialization of agriculture and food manufacture as well as the commercialization of food trade and marketing on an unprecedented scale. The world witnessed massive increases in the production of staples, fruits and vegetables, edible oils, dairy products, meat, fish and manufactured foods. In countries like India, the coupling of the 'Green Revolution' (rice and wheat) and 'White Revolution' (milk and dairy products) appeared to end food scarcity and promised to prevent malnutrition.

Globally, transnational food trade scaled up commercial marketing of agricultural products and manufactured food products. Yet, malnutrition continued to manifest in many forms. Some forms arose due to inadequate food availability to poorer sections of the population while others arose from inappropriate diets that created an imbalance of calories and nutrients in many persons.

Challenge of the Future

The demand for food will rise over the next thirty years due to an increase in the size of the world population, change of demographic profile in that population (as people live longer and consume more food over lifetime as adults), increasing urbanization (accompanied by greater consumption) and reduced poverty levels (enabling higher spending capacity on food). At the same time, the production of food will decrease due to the impact of climate change on agriculture and livestock and the reduction of land available for farming due to population growth.

It is projected that the demand for food will increase by 14 per cent per decade, while the production of food will fall by 2 per cent per decade. Compared to 2000, the world will need 60 per cent more food to feed a population of 9 billion in 2050. The global food systems will face a major challenge, unless collective efforts are made to find sustainable solutions.[2]

We will need to produce more food per unit investment of land, water and energy. Even as we endeavour to produce more food for the growing global population, we need to ensure that it meets the nutritional needs of the people with the right balance of nutrients provided by dietary diversity.

It is also necessary to produce, market and consume this food in an environmentally sustainable manner. Otherwise, we will perpetuate a mutually detrimental relationship where agriculture and food systems damage the environment and environmental degradation will, in turn, adversely affect the quantity and quality of food production.

Environmentally Sustainable Food Systems

According to the United Nation, Food and Agriculture Organization (FAO), even as of now, food systems are responsible for up to 29 per cent of total greenhouse gas emissions. Agriculture accounts for 70 per cent of the world's water use and is responsible for 80 per cent of global deforestation.[3] While some of this has to be viewed as unavoidable due to the essentiality of agriculture for human nutrition, health and survival, future agriculture and food systems have to become efficient in producing more food per unit of land, water and energy utilized. At the same time, the nutrient quality of foods produced and consumed have to be more attuned to the promotion and protection of human health.

Food production, distribution and consumption are complex activities that involve several human interactions in a chain of connected initiatives. Agricultural production, even in mechanized systems, involves human beings working as teams to carry out a series of activities, from planting to harvesting. The transformation of crops into food products involves many human efforts. At any of these steps, the nutrient quality of food can be altered in a manner that can be damaging to health.

Sometimes, there are unintended consequences. When India launched its 'Green Revolution' in the 1960s to overcome food shortages, newer high-yield varieties of rice and wheat were introduced. North Indian states became the large granaries of India. Deforestation and irrigation canals, initiated in the British era, were already environmental threats. When double cropping was introduced as an annual pattern during the Green Revolution, groundwater was tapped to feed the water-thirsty crops.

As groundwater was getting depleted, laws were enacted forbidding farmers to sow and transplant paddy before the anticipated date of the monsoon. This was to avoid the depletion of groundwater in the hot summer months through agricultural operations. This reduced the inter-crop interval. When the first crop was harvested, farmers did not have sufficient time before planting the second crop to completely pluck out the earlier crop's waste before the next crop is planted. The waste was burnt, to quickly clear the field for planting the next crop. This has, in recent years, aggravated air pollution to dangerously high levels in the months of October and November in Northern India.

The shift to high-yielding varieties of rice and wheat also resulted in a reduction in the production of nutritious crops like pulses and millets. This adversely affected dietary diversity and the nutrient quality of food. Obesity and diabetes rates in the population went up. The processing of grain also led to highly polished varieties replacing coarse grains, which were stripped of fibre and some other essential nutrients in the process. The 'glycaemic index' of the food increased, as a result, again predisposing their consumer to diabetes. Thus, what set out to be a well-intended initiative to improve food security and reduce hunger turned out to have unanticipated adverse consequences for health and the environment.

Increased consumption of animal foods has resulted in factory farms of cattle and poultry being established. Agricultural land is cleared to breed cattle or used to grow grain to feed commercially bred animals. The FAO estimates that if all persons on earth gave up animal-sourced foods and switched to plant-based foods, the land required for agriculture would be 76 per cent less![4] This is true for a vegan diet as well as for a diet that has plants, eggs and fish only. Even if this is not achieved, less dependence on animal foods and higher consumption of plant foods will reduce the risk of cardiovascular diseases, cancers, diabetes and obesity while protecting the environment and diminishing the dangers of zoonotic pandemics and antimicrobial resistance.

Grain-fed animals have a different fatty acid composition in their meat than grass-fed animals, with the former being more likely to cause atherosclerosis of blood vessels. The risk of heart attacks and strokes rises with the consumption of grain-fed meat, in comparison to grass-fed meat. Antibiotics are also extensively used in animal breeding, contributing to the rising threat of anti-microbial resistance. Of global antibiotic consumption, human use accounts for 30 per cent, while veterinary use contributes to 70 per cent.

Reorienting Food Systems

Agriculture and food systems have, over the past century, become increasingly disconnected from the principal objective of providing a calorically adequate and nutritionally appropriate diet to every person, at each stage of life. Instead, they became captive to commercial interests, initially farmer's lobbies and later to agribusiness industries. Large-scale production of foods that earn profits by creating customer cravings became the practice, even if the food products were grossly mismatched to healthy nutrition. Since large volumes of production became the guiding principle of commerce, environmental concerns about forestry and water conservation were brushed away.

The growing clout of the commercial interests also brought forth price subsidies and environmental exemptions. The corporatization of the food business led to shareholder interests preventing any switch from profit-making unhealthy food products and beverages to healthier products. Regulatory attempts to reduce the levels of refined sugar, salt and unhealthy fats in manufactured foods were met with stiff resistance. The increasingly transnational character of the food industry has also created a growing market in most countries, for unhealthy food products, replacing traditional diets and nutrient-rich foods.

To change the complex, commercialized, environmentally damaging and health-unfriendly food and agriculture systems, we need several measures. Regulatory measures (fiscal, legal and administrative) can curb the marketing of unhealthy foods. Fiscal interventions (like higher taxes) can increase the price and reduce the consumption of calorie-loaded but nutrient-poor ultra-processed foods and sugary drinks, while subsidies and lower taxes can increase the production and consumption of healthier crops and food products. Consumer consciousness, promoted through increased health and nutrition literacy in the population, can reset the production and supply dynamics through increased demand for healthy foods in preference to unhealthy foods.

Within countries, a combination of government action and consumer behaviour can reset industry behaviour. Public financing, involving government spending, is a major purchaser of food in many countries. From schools to hospitals, government offices and industries to the army and police, and prisons to public distribution systems for subsidized food supply to many sections of the public, the government is often a big spender and a prized customer of the food industry. By clearly indicating a preference for purchasing healthier food products and avoiding spending on unhealthy food products, the government can strongly nudge the food and agriculture industry to produce and market products that promote health and protect the environment. Consumers can exert pressure on the industry as well as the government, the former as customers and the latter as voters.

Transnational trade would need to be regulated to prevent dumping of unhealthy food products in the markets of low- and middle-income countries. The agriculture and food industries must recognize the health, environmental and social costs of producing and promoting unhealthy products and profit from the long-term dividends of a healthier global population living in a more environmentally secure world. Global trade agreements can influence the patterns of trade if, instead of protecting industry interests, they protect the public interest. The World Trade Organization (WTO) would be a good place for governments to demonstrate that political will. Free market tents, mostly favouring the food industry, have guided WTO policies. Rich countries have used their political muscle to push through trade agreements that favour their industries. The sooner they realize that harmful agricultural and food industry practices pose a major threat to global health, environment and sustainable development, the better it will be for global nutrition. The political economy of global health and nutrition has to change if the young persons of today have to live in a better world.

All of these would require the collective will and concerted action by many people across the world. So, we must recognize that our nutrition and health are connected to complex systems that require us to act at a societal level. This is an essential need not only to protect ourselves but also to ensure that we create food and agriculture systems that are health promoting for future generations too.

PART III

Social, Economic and Commercial Determinants

'Health inequalities and the social determinants of health
are not a footnote to the determinants of health. They are
the main issue.'*

—MICHAEL MARMOT

---

* 'Michael Marmot.', *BMJ: British Medical Journal*, 2015, 6.

Water Security and Sanitation Services

> 'You will never solve poverty without solving water and sanitation.'
>
> —MATT DAMON

From early on in human existence, the availability of fresh water to drink has been recognized as essential to life. Ponds and pools, streams and rivers provided this resource to early humans. Then came the wells and canals. Ancient civilizations grew near rivers. Fortunately, the water was mostly uncontaminated. Even ancient townships of the Indus Valley civilization had hydraulic pipes for water supply and public drainage systems to which drains from houses were connected. This is perhaps the first known instance of water and sanitation engineering in the history of human habitats.

Later, the challenges of water pollution and admixture with sewage started posing health threats. This became particularly threatening as cities grew to house people in crowded spaces. The Sanitary Movement began in England in the 1830s, through the energetic efforts of Edwin Chadwick,[1] and spread to other European cities. The need to clear sewage and garbage, while ensuring the supply of clean drinking water, became a strong article of urban planning and governance as cities were cleaned up. Unfortunately, the class interests of feudal societies separated the crowded poor from the richer sections, and challenges of water and sanitation persisted for the poor as cities grew.

The beginning of public health-related investigations linking water and sanitation to disease outbreaks is often dated to 1854, when John Snow,[2] a British doctor, identified the source of a cholera outbreak in London to a water pump in Broad Street, which was yielding water contaminated with sewage. Initially scoffed at by civic authorities and other doctors, Snow received unlikely support (and valuable clues) from a preacher, Reverend Whitehead, who had initially begun an investigation of his own to prove Snow wrong.

Science was well served by the generation of a hypothesis and systematic data-gathering attempts to both prove and refute it. Philosopher of science Karl Popper would have approved of the method! Removal of the pump handle in Broad Street ended the cholera epidemic and gave a fillip to public health engineering.

Continuing Lack of Access

Unfortunately, access to clean drinking water is still unavailable to many in the world. According to the United Nations, one out of three persons worldwide does not have access to clean drinking water.[3] Two out of three do not have access to a hand-washing facility with soap and water. Around 892 million persons practice open defecation.[4] More than 80 per cent of wastewater resulting from human activities is discharged into rivers or seas without any removal of pollutants.

It has been estimated that 4 per cent of all global deaths and 5.7 per cent of disability-adjusted life years lost worldwide result from poor access to water, sanitation and hygiene.[5] Lack of clean drinking water and poor sanitation result in many infectious diseases. Cholera, diarrhoea, dysentery, typhoid fever, infective hepatitis, amoebiasis and giardiasis are among the many diseases that are spread through poor sanitation and contaminated water.

Besides human excreta contributing to biological pollutants, chemical pollutants from industrial effluents also contaminate the rivers and add to the dangers to human health. As soil and water get contaminated by human and animal excreta, worm infestations also increase. Hook worm, round worm, tapeworm and pin worm are among these parasitic worm infestations.

Even when the water is clean, there are dangers to health from increasing water scarcity. The human body is composed mostly of water. While the average is stated to be around 60 per cent of the body weight, the proportion varies with age, gender, ambient temperature and state of health. Infants have up to 75–80 per cent of their body weight composed of water. Adult males have around 60–65 per cent and adult females have around 50–55 per cent on average.[6] This is why infants are far more vulnerable to a hot ambient temperature—a danger we must be wary of as global warming pushes the mercury to ever-higher degrees.

Water is essential for many bodily functions. It forms part of our body fluids, including the bloodstream. It lubricates our joints, regulates body temperature and maintains blood pressure. It helps carry excreta out of the body, clearing it of many toxins. It also aids us in cleaning ourselves and in cooking our food. It irrigates the fields that produce the food that nourishes our body. It then enters the body through the foods we consume.

The scarcity of water can harm human health in many ways. The danger of diminishing water supply in different parts of the world is a threat to human health and survival. Such shortages will be accentuated with the growth of the global population, leading to forebodings of 'water wars' in the future.

Targets to Reach

Goal 6 of the Sustainable Development Goals (SDGs) adopted by the United Nations in 2015 calls on the global community to ensure access to water and sanitation for all by 2030. It sets out several targets:[7]

- By 2030, achieve universal and equitable access to safe and affordable drinking water for all

- By 2030, achieve access to adequate and equitable sanitation and hygiene for all and end open defecation, paying special attention to the needs of women and girls and those in vulnerable situations

- By 2030, improve water quality by reducing pollution, eliminating dumping and minimizing the release of hazardous chemicals and materials, halving the proportion of untreated wastewater and substantially increasing recycling and safe reuse globally

- By 2030, substantially increase water-use efficiency across all sectors and ensure sustainable withdrawals and supply of freshwater to address water scarcity and substantially reduce the number of people suffering from water scarcity

- By 2030, implement integrated water resources management at all levels, including through transboundary cooperation as appropriate

- By 2020, protect and restore water-related ecosystems, including mountains, forests, wetlands, rivers, aquifers and lakes

In many low- and middle-income countries, progress towards these goals is slow. COVID-19 has occupied the attention of most countries since January 2020. The irony lies in the fact that one of the key public health measures advocated for protection against infection by the SARS CoV-2 virus is frequent hand washing. In many communities, water has been a scarce commodity for daily necessities. Frequent hand washing amounts to impractical advice in such situations. Governments and municipal authorities must recognize this contradiction between such advice and availability, to initiate and implement urgent measures for providing a protected water supply in adequate quantities to all communities.

What Can We Do?

Here again, the ability to adopt healthy behaviours and protect one's health lies beyond the personal capability of any individual. We depend on organized civic systems to get clean drinking water from taps. We are deprived of adequate supply when civic administrations do not plan and execute well to deliver water or when commercial entities usurp huge amounts of water to bottle as sold water or convert to a variety of beverages.

We are deprived of water when large amounts are diverted for captive animal breeding for meat production and for water-hungry crops like tobacco that have no nutritive value. The water crisis will only grow more acute with a rise in global warming.

Response to the water crisis requires collective societal resolve. This has to happen at the village, municipal, national and global levels and involves many measures for water conservation, equitable distribution, avoidance of wastage and appropriate usage to meet health and nutrition goals. These varied but complementary measures are beyond the capacity of any single human but can be achieved if we pursue common goals through concerted action. We need to stay connected!

Economic Development and Health: Growth and Equity

'An imbalance between rich and poor is the oldest and most fatal ailment of all republics.'[1]

—PLUTARCH

Over the past two centuries, human life expectancy has doubled in most parts of the world. Much of this is attributable to economic development that translates into improved social conditions, food security, better healthcare and greater access to education, which by itself has a powerful positive impact on health. The sanitary environment too usually improves with economic development, though the larger physical environment may be degraded by economic policies that are insensitive to conservation and environmental protection. Healthcare systems improve with greater investment in infrastructure, personnel, equipment, drugs, technologies and research that spurs discovery, development and delivery of products that foster health.

Health and Equitable Economic Growth

It has been widely recognized for a long time that economic growth spurs improved health in a population. It was quantitatively assessed and graphically presented as the Millennium Curve by Preston in 1972.[2] The curve revealed that life expectancy grows sharply with per capita income increase, till it starts plateauing around 5000 dollars per capita (in purchasing power at that time). Further gains in income produce only small incremental gains in life expectancy. So, as countries lift themselves out of poverty, the life expectancy of their people increases till a stable level of economic growth levels off that effect.

However, the gain in life expectancy (at any level of income rise) is conditioned by the level of income equality and social equality in that society. This was clearly demonstrated by Richard Wilkinson and Kate Pickering in their book, *The Spirit Level*.[3] Countries at the same level of per capita income have differing levels of life expectancy and indicators of well-being, depending on the within-population gradient in their per capita incomes.

Countries with large income gaps within their population have lower gains from economic growth and comparable average per capita income levels than countries with a narrower gap, reflecting a higher level of equity. Other forms of inequality too (as in educational opportunities, gender discrimination or racial prejudice) extract a price in the health status of the society, which falls behind the potential high predicted by the level of economic development.

Inequality within societies affects the health of not only the poor but also the rich. It has been observed that the rich in unequal societies have worse health outcomes than their counterparts in more equal societies, even after adjusting for income levels. This is easily understandable for infectious diseases that can spread from the poor, who are more vulnerable, to the rich who cannot completely escape the exposure.

However, even stressful conditions, violence and addictions, which are products of unequal societies and damage the health of the poor, can also affect the rich in that society. Unless equality is promoted as a core value, by economic and social systems, the health of that population will lag behind the level of economic development, impacting the poor the most but not sparing the rich.

Bidirectional Relationship between Health and Economic Status

The relationship between health and economic status is bidirectional, both in populations and in individuals. Healthy populations are more productive and accelerate economic development. Health promotion and disease prevention reduce the risk of serious disease or delay its onset till a very elderly age, reducing healthcare costs.

Preventing public health emergencies prevent national and global economies from being derailed. The health sector also creates many jobs, which is good for the economy. If families avoid the need of high healthcare costs or countries can reduce spending on costly clinical care, money so saved can be spent on other purchases for the family or other developmental projects by the government, thereby stimulating economic growth.

Several global reports of the last three decades have emphasized the economic benefits of investing in the health of the populations. Prior to that, healthcare was often regarded by economists as a socially necessary but economically unproductive expenditure, in conventional economic thinking. William Baumol, an influential economist of the twentieth century, had even described healthcare as a 'cost disease' that failed to generate economic returns commensurate with the investment unlike the industrial engines of economic growth. However, the WHO Commission on Macroeconomics of Health (2001)[4] and two Commissions on Investing in Health (1993, 2013)[5] provided clear and convincing evidence of population health as an accelerator of economic development. The last named commission estimated that every dollar invested in health would yield a nine-fold return in low income countries and a twenty-fold return in middle income countries.

At the level of the individual, poverty opens the gate to illness while illness can push a person into poverty. A poor person is at a greater risk of illness due to poor diet, inadequate housing, unsanitary surroundings, low levels of education and health literacy, risk-prone employment, hindered access to healthcare or inability to afford it. When a person who is just above the poverty line becomes ill, the cost of healthcare and lost wages push that person into poverty.

If a person whose income is the source of a family's economic security loses employment due to disease or disability, or dies due to severe illness, the family too becomes the victim of economic adversity. Nutrition and healthcare are compromised for the whole family and education of children may be abruptly ended pushing them into child labour. The stress of poverty also takes a severe toll on mental health.

Poverty creating ill health has been well recognized in the case of infectious diseases like childhood diarrhoea, tuberculosis or nutritional deficiency disorders like anaemia or stunting. Maternal mortality and child mortality too are higher in poor countries and among poor persons within a country. However, non-communicable diseases (NCDs) such as cardiovascular, respiratory, and kidney disorders, diabetes and cancers were for long considered to be diseases of affluence and not a problem for the poor. Such an impression led to their being left out of the Millennium Development Goals (MDGs) in 2000.

However, compelling evidence has emerged over the past quarter century that the poor among countries and the poor within countries are increasingly emerging as the most vulnerable victims of NCDs. Indeed, evidence came forth even in the last quarter of the twentieth century that the social gradient had reversed in high-income countries compared to mid-century patterns of disease in their populations. Whether in Europe or North America, the poor and the near-poor had a clearly evident higher burden of NCDs since the 1980s. This pattern later extended to middle-income countries and is now manifesting in many low-income countries too.

The reversal of the social gradient for NCDs is driven by the pattern of economic development. As economic growth raises per capita incomes, the purchasing power of persons rises even in the lower socio-economic groups though they are still far from affluence. When the mediators of risk become mass produced for mass consumption, those goods become more affordable.

As aspirational lifestyles are marketed aggressively, unhealthy foods, tobacco and alcohol become the preferred purchases of the expanding middle class and even attract the poor. At this time, the rich and the more educated sections would have become more aware of products and practices that increase the risk of NCDs, through better access to emerging scientific knowledge. They would change their living habits for the better, giving up tobacco, eating more fruit and vegetables and undertaking more physical activity in sports and gyms or on jogging tracks.

The poor may not have access to that level of health information. Even if they do, their financial status does not permit them to purchase healthy edible oils, plenty of fruit and vegetables, gym memberships or home treadmills. As safe cycling lanes and pedestrian paths shrink in the growing metros of low- and middle-income countries, physical activity levels plummet for the poor who use mechanized mass transport.

At the same time, tobacco and fast food industries target the demographic groups who are experiencing a slight rise in their incomes with the imagery of aspirational lifestyles prominently positioning their products. This, coupled with low levels of health literacy, propel lower socio-economic groups into the vortex of high-risk behaviours and risk factors for NCDs. Is it any wonder that the prevalence of obesity and cardiovascular disease is now most frequent in low-income groups in the USA and the UK?

The reversal of the social gradient for different NCD risk factors, in response to economic and commercial influences, does not happen simultaneously for all risk factors within a population. Tobacco habit is usually the first to reverse, with the rich giving it up or avoiding it because of known risks, while the poor are enticed into the addiction with cunningly targeted marketing and cheaper products. High blood pressure is the next risk factor to reverse, as the salt content of the diet increases. Changes in blood fat composition and levels follow as dietary patterns change. Physical activity levels reduce and diabetes becomes more manifest.

Overt obesity follows later in this calendar of social gradient reversal, even though abdominal obesity would have preceded it, appearing alongside the changes in blood fats and blood sugar. Such patterns of progressively reversing social gradients become evident when we compare countries of Africa, Asia and Latin America, which are at different stages of developmental transition, both on their current risk factor profiles and on time trends over the past three decades.

The poor also face greater difficulties in accessing healthcare, because of both healthcare system failures and the constraints of their working conditions which do not permit them the time to seek care due to fear of losing wages. When they do seek care, they frequently face stigma and discrimination from healthcare providers. The financial cost of repeated visits to healthcare facilities, long-term medication and periodically prescribed diagnostic tests, during medical follow-ups, become unaffordable to them. The diseases associated with poverty become aggravated by the absence of accessible and affordable care. The lives of the poor are short-changed as a result.

Economic inequality is growing in the world:

- The Multi-Dimensional Poverty Index counted 1.3 billion people (23 per cent) across 101 countries to be poor, with half that number to be under 18 years of age.

  (United Nations Development Programme, 2019)[6]

- The world's 2153 billionaires have more wealth than the 4.6 billion people who are from the bottom 60 per cent of the global population.

  (Oxfam Report on Global Poverty, 2020)[7]

- Gini Index is a measure of income distribution across income percentiles of a population. The higher the Gini index, the greater is the inequality. The Gini index in Japan was 29.9 per cent in 2019. In the USA, it was 48.5 per cent. Life expectancy in Japan in 2020 is 84.6 years. In the USA, it is 78.9 years.

- The wealth of the world's ten richest men has doubled since the COVID-19 pandemic began. The incomes of 99 per cent of humanity are worse off because of COVID-19.

  (Inequality Kills: Oxfam International, January 2022)[8]

All nations must seek greater economic development to advance human development, of which health is a vital component. Low-income countries will benefit the most in terms of such health gains.[11] However, income inequalities exist in all countries to a varying extent. Where large inequalities exist, the benefits of economic development are diminished.

In highly unequal societies, the health of the rich too does not reflect the economic status, as inequality extracts a price from all sections of that society. To reap optimal health benefits from economic development, inequality must be reduced. Poverty is an abomination that cannot be allowed to persist in a civilized society, for many moral reasons but also for the protection of human health.

Education and Health: A Close Relationship

'I feel that we can't educate children who are not healthy, and we can't keep them healthy if they're not educated. There has to be a marriage between health and education. You can't learn if your mind is full of unhealthy images from daily life and confusion about right and wrong.'[1]

—JOYCELYN ELDERS

Education or health? COVID-19 planted a cruel question for educators and public health experts to brood over. For two years, schools and colleges in most parts of the world were closed. The reasons offered were that viral transmission was to be curtailed and young persons were both vulnerable to infection and could become active agents in infecting vulnerable adults because of their high mobility. This had to be considered against the loss of education, which is well recognized to be an important agent for promoting health among individuals and populations.

What would be the delayed health effects of interrupted education? Besides, of course, the immediate COVID-19 related effects on mental health, through isolation and lack of socialization with peers in a period of heightened anxiety, fear and grief? Or the rise in child obesity levels stoked by anxiety-driven overeating of junk foods and enforced physical inactivity?

Education: A Positive Influence on Health

It is an axiom of public health that education improves the health of societies and protects the health of individuals. 'A good quality education is the foundation of health and well-being. For people to lead healthy and productive lives, they need knowledge to prevent sickness and disease.' This is a declaration by the United Nations Educational, Scientific and Cultural Organization (UNESCO) that further affirms that 'education is a catalyst for development and a health intervention in its own right'.[2]

The Incheon Declaration of 2015 on Sustainable Development Goal 4[3] affirms that education endows the skills, values and attitudes that enable citizens to lead healthy and fulfilled lives and make informed decisions. In a bidirectional relationship, ill health impedes access to education and the attainment of knowledge and skills.

There is a wealth of evidence, from comparisons within and across countries, that bears out these assertions on the positive impact of education on the health status of individuals and populations. Higher levels of education usually provide greater access to health-related information which, when assimilated and stored as knowledge, can promote and sustain healthy behaviours. Education also increases opportunities for higher-income-earning employment. Better economic status, in turn, enables a person to afford more nutritious and safe food, live in better housing with the assurance of clean water and sanitation and amidst healthier physical and climatic surroundings.

Higher income, coupled with good education, also enables one to access better healthcare. Health-seeking behaviours, insurance literacy, ability to engage in participatory decision-making with the treating doctor, adherence to treatment and capacity for self-care are all better with higher levels of education. Worldwide, unhealthy behaviours such as tobacco consumption and alcohol abuse are negatively correlated with educational status. Such social gradients, across the levels of education, are most evident within individual countries while other differences dilute the association when different countries are compared.

Education Has Even Greater Impact than Income

While education and income often go together as positive determinants of health, education has a greater impact on health than income. Even a financially well-off person will not make healthy choices related to food, exercise or addictive behaviours, if education does not provide the requisite knowledge. On the other hand, an educated person is likelier to adopt healthy behaviours and make healthy food choices, even within the constraints of limited income.

At any given level of income, higher education offers better health protection. Ideally, healthy behaviours are most likely to be adopted when health literacy and analytic ability provided by education are supported by lowering of financial and access barriers to health-promoting agents and environments.

However, these relationships are not wholly independent, always linear or universal. The people of Hunza valley, with a host of centenarians, are healthy not because of high educational attainment but because of a pristine environment and healthy traditional diets.[4] Other communities too derive health benefits from traditional diets, including herbal medicines.

In such cases, it is not the knowledge gained through formal education that promotes and protects health but tacit knowledge and experiential wisdom that provides the health benefit. While knowledge is gained most easily and widely from structured formal education, there are also other channels for acquiring health-friendly knowledge. Mass media also help to quickly disseminate health-relevant knowledge to a large number of persons whose formal education may be varied.

Social Media, Formal and Informal Channels of Education

The positive relationship of education with health was clearly evident in the twentieth century. However, the rapid growth of social media in the twenty-first century is blurring the benefit. The best-case scenario is of widespread rise in health and nutrition literacy through print, electronic and social media. While it is happening to some extent, the infiltration of fake news and anti-science propaganda into social media has proved harmful in the adoption of healthy behaviours. This has been painfully evident during the COVID-19 pandemic. Highly educated persons became prejudiced purveyors and deluded victims of false information, while less educated people were willing to trust government health workers.

For education, formal and informal, to result in knowledge that positively impacts health behaviours of a large number of people, we need to both raise the level of formal education by improving its access and quality and fast track health and nutrition literacy among the general population. The content of educational messages must be well founded on sound science, while taking into account the specific health needs and cultural practices of the population groups being addressed. Credible agencies and individuals must be engaged to quickly counter and contain fake news. The power of education can then be used to promote the health of populations and protect the health of individuals.

Educational Institutions and Students

Educational institutions can transform students into agents of health promotion. School and college students who are sensitized to health issues and motivated to adopt healthy behaviours at the personal level can also become change agents in the family, neighbourhood and the wider community. Health-promoting schools begin by changing their own environment, by ensuring clean water, good sanitation, adequate ventilation, playgrounds, ban on use of tobacco products (by students and school personnel) and by providing healthy food choices and beverages in school meals and cafeteria.

An educated and engaged younger generation can power health transformation in the country. There are several examples, from different countries, of young persons from schools and colleges leading movements for environmental protection, access to medicines, tobacco control, road safety and gender equity.

In India too, HRIDAY (Health Related Information Dissemination Among Youth) and SHAN (Student Health Action Network) have worked in schools to promote life-skills education by combining health literacy and informed health advocacy.[5]

The former enabled teacher-assisted, peer-led health education for younger school students (learning the fact) while the latter catalysed advocacy by older students to align multi-sectoral policies to the health needs of society (learning to act). Several global youth meets on health, environment and sustainable development were also organized.

If education and health are to benefit from a synergistic relationship to advance human development, interactions and alliances are needed between many persons and organizations. This endeavour is a collective social responsibility. Individualism will not achieve the progress we need. So, we need to keep connected, locally and globally.

Discrimination Creates Health Inequality

'Of all the forms of inequality, injustice in healthcare is the most shocking and inhumane.'[1]

—MARTIN LUTHER KING JR.

Congenial social relations extending across society and mutually supportive social groups in communities have been shown to benefit the health of individuals whose lives are affected by those inter-personal connections. Discrimination and hostility that any section of society is subjected to undermines the physical and mental health of individuals who are the victims of prejudice and persecution. These associations demonstrate how our health is connected to the social dynamics of the world we live in.

Discrimination exists in many forms, with diverse social groups as victims. Gender, race, religion, ethnicity, poverty, educational attainment, occupation, social status and political beliefs are among the factors that are used as the basis for unfair and even hurtful treatment of people. These restrict the pathways through which individuals can promote and protect their health, while also impeding their ability to access health services needed to restore health when they fall sick.

Gender

Gender has been an area of discrimination for millennia, even when the label was used only to differentiate the sex assigned at birth. Gender roles were assigned for life, which promoted male domination and made women victims of patriarchy. Even as it became clear that sexual preferences could sometimes involve same-sex relationships and transgender identities were preferred by some, the labels attached at birth continued to dominate thinking and differentiate people in a binary mode.

Within this binary construct of male and female, gender assigned roles defined the lives of boys and girls, men and women. These have had a bearing on the health of people whose gender placed them at a disadvantage. When we consider groups that identify themselves in a non-binary mode as lesbian, gay, bisexual, transsexual, queer, intersex or asexual (LGBTQIA), there are also other forms of discrimination that have adverse effects on health. A society that accepts differences and accommodates diversity can enable all of its members to promote and protect their health.

Women start life with some biological advantages, where evolutionary safeguards provided by nature for survival of the human species confer higher life expectancy on them than observed in males. For instance, immune systems are intrinsically stronger and risk of a heart attack before menopause is lower in women than in men of same age.[2] However, these biological advantages are undermined and nullified by several adversities of social circumstances that women face in many parts of the world.

Preference for a male child can lead to female foeticide or infanticide. Even when a female baby lives, gender preference coupled with poverty results in underfed girl babies. An undernourished girl child grows into an anaemic adolescent and underweight woman who is often rushed into early marriage and teen pregnancy. Childbirth becomes hazardous for the young woman whose body and mind are unprepared for motherhood.[3] The smaller pelvic size of an undernourished mother makes childbirth difficult, while the small-sized placenta limits nourishment to the baby. Even if an undernourished baby is born alive and survives, several health problems will impede that child's development.

Restricted opportunities, for education and employment, limit women's economic independence and decision-making autonomy, while promoting male dominance. This has an impact on a woman's physical and mental health. From the type of food she eats to the kind of healthcare she gets, a lot is dependent on the decisions made by the male members of the family. Male addictions subject her to domestic violence while male promiscuity makes her the victim of sexually transmitted diseases.[4]

In some societies, female genital mutilation is practised while in others access to contraception is impeded. Rape and other forms of sexual violence inflict physical and mental trauma on many, age being no bar. While such a canvas of discrimination and oppression certainly does not portray the picture of all women in all societies, even some women suffering such a fate anywhere cannot be countenanced in a civilized society that values the health and well-being of all its members.

Environmental determinants too act adversely against women in some ways. In several countries of South Asia and Africa,[5] rural women who do not have ready and affordable access to cooking gas or electric stoves use biomass fuels of wood which they gather and burn in the kitchen. For them, the baby in their arms or the toddler playing around them, the fumes from the burning biomass become the kitchen's curse. This indoor air pollution causes respiratory problems (chronic obstructive airway disease and asthma), hypertension, cardiovascular disease, diabetes and cancers among the many adverse health effects.[6] This happens through both direct cytotoxic and inflammatory effects as well as epigenetic modifications. Where domestic water supply is not available, women are forced to fetch water from far, experiencing physical exhaustion, heat stress, risking wild animal or snake attacks and even sexual attacks from predatory males. Absence of household toilets also forces women to risk physical danger by performing ablutions outdoors away from home.

Not infrequently, such disadvantages are compounded by multiple adversities. A girl born in a poor family, belonging to a minority group, not having means to be educated or getting employed and having a physical disability has the dice loaded against her. Unless social structures change to remove many of the disadvantages and provide suitable assistance to deal with others, such a girl would find it difficult to experience health and well-being in any meaningful measure.

Healthy gender relations are vital for a healthy society.[7] Gender respect is an essential requirement for promoting gender equity, not as a concession but out of conviction. Male and female stereotypes need to be erased from the minds of children and young persons, even as sexual identities get defined and any person seeks an emotional or physical relationship with another person, whatever be the preferred gender identity of either person. This cannot be seen merely as a cultural construct or a civilizational code but as a necessary element of the physical and mental health of all members of society, whatever their gender identity and sexual orientation. This understanding, free from prejudice and discrimination, must be fostered from childhood so that children, and the adults that they grow into, connect as emotionally empathetic human beings and not as gendered stereotypes seeking dominance and displaying disrespect.

For long, the medical profession was dominated by male doctors. Even in medical research, many clinical trials included only male patients. Clinical findings, diagnostic tests and treatments found appropriate for males were automatically applied to women. It was only later, when it became clear that men and women differed in clinical presentations and treatment responses in several disorders, including coronary heart disease, that clinical trials started mandating the inclusion of women.[8]

An increase in the number of women researchers too improved the scale and quality of research done on women's health conditions in allopathic medicine. Traditional systems of medicine were more sensitive to gender differences in disease symptomatology and treatments. Mostly, however, male patriarchy dominated the field of medicine for far too long, doing injustice to women's health.

Poverty

Julian Tudor Hart proposed the Inverse Care Law in 1971. The law, as originally stated, reads: 'The availability of good medical care tends to vary inversely with the need for it in the population served.' He went to explain that this law 'operates more completely where medical care is exposed to market forces, and less so where such exposure is reduced.'[9] He declared that when healthcare becomes a commodity, rich people get lots of it and poor people do not get any of it.

It has been clearly shown, in studies conducted across many countries, that healthcare available to poorer sections of the community is poor in quality and also frequently comes at an unaffordable price.[10] The poor have lower educational levels, with inadequate health literacy. This diminishes the quality of self-care, while impeding health-seeking behaviours. The poor cannot purchase good quality healthcare if they are not protected by a system of universal health coverage. Even if free care is available, social prejudice against a poorly dressed person, who is unable to converse in a polished manner, often results in limited attention and suboptimal care. In contrast the rich and other social elites expect, demand and invariably get respectful attention and good quality care from a healthcare team.

Poverty not only predisposes a person to disease but also detracts from the quality of healthcare, leaving the poor doubly disadvantaged. The preferential treatment given to the rich and social elites follows the biblical Matthew principle that 'for unto everyone that hath shall be given, and he shall have abundance: but from that hath not, shall be taken away, even that which he hath.'[11] Frequently, even healthcare services provided by the government are subject to 'elite capture', while the poor who receive inadequate services are further impoverished.

In countries where contributory health insurance and privately purchased healthcare are the principal modes of payment for healthcare services, the poor are at great disadvantage. Poverty not only breeds ill health but also makes healthcare unaffordable. Such systems discriminate against the poor. However, the society as a whole suffers because of the spread of infectious diseases, reduced productivity and disrupted social harmony due to addictive behaviours. While it is essential to reduce poverty, it is also necessary to ensure that health services do not discriminate against the poor.

Race, Ethnicity, Geography, Language, Culture

One of the tragedies of human history has been the manner in which the 'other' has been identified as an object of derision, suspicion, fear or unjustified hate. It has an impact on the mental and even physical health of both the vilifier and the vilified. Negative emotions raise blood pressure, trigger inflammation and depress immunity. The object of discrimination, which may even extend to oppression, suffers even more negative consequences. Healthcare services are often unavailable or are of poor quality.

Race as a determinant of the quality of healthcare has long been debated in the USA. People of colour have received poorer healthcare over centuries. Even during the recent COVID-19 pandemic, such instances were frequently reported. It was a discrimination that went beyond occupation or income. While in hospital as a patient of COVID-19, Doctor Susan Moore complained in a recorded video that she was treated with indifference by a white doctor and her complaints were ignored because she was black. She died later.[12]

The *New York Times* commented that 'voluminous research suggests that Black patients often receive treatment inferior to their white counterparts'.[13] The fact that Moore was a medical doctor herself did not help to breach prejudice. Even in India, persons from scheduled tribes, who have the worst health indicators among various socio-demographic groups, receive suboptimal healthcare. Indigenous peoples in the USA, Canada and Australia have also been recipients of poor healthcare services.

Similarly, religious affiliations, linguistic differences and provincial labels can become the basis for discrimination in healthcare services, from employment of healthcare workers to attitudes and behaviour towards patients and their attendants. This can undermine the availability and quality of healthcare. This is an unfortunate phenomenon witnessed in many countries.

Migration and Conflict

During most of the twentieth century, migration was motivated by the desire to seek new opportunities for education, employment and better living conditions. It was not a forced migration due to conflict or climate change. In most cases, the migrants were also welcomed in the recipient countries as they brought young and healthy individuals to add to the productive workforce of the countries of adoption. If the migrants were students, they contributed to the income of the universities. Scientists, innovative technologists, entrepreneurs, writers and sportspersons migrated to add to the wealth of the USA, UK and Europe. While migration of healthcare workers had a negative impact on the home countries, the recipient countries benefited. The health of migrants was never in jeopardy due to xenophobia and violence.

However, the twenty-first century has seen a large spurt in forced migration, mostly due to conflict but also due to climate change. This has resulted in injuries, disease and death on the migration routes. Poignant pictures of children drowning on unsafe boat journeys and migrants suffocating to death in jam-packed trucks became all too frequent visuals in news media. The plight of children separated from parents and held in custody on the US–Mexico border challenged humanity's claim to high values and noble conduct as the hallmark of our advancing civilization. Europe has seen truckers stuck in a UK–France standoff, while boat tragedies claimed lives in the sea between the two countries.[14] The border between Poland and Belarus became a tinderbox with mass migrants.[15]

Even migrants who have survived a perilous journey are often treated as unwelcome intruders and barricaded in crowded shelters. Countries that colonized others without compunction in the past, through armies and trade, now regard even a humanitarian emergency as weak grounds to welcome desperate migrants. Conditions are never conducive to the health of humans in such situations.

Sectarian strife and wars claimed many lives in West Asia, Africa and South Asia. Religious extremism spread violence worldwide and wars were triggered by external interventions aiming to bring about 'regime change'. Military coups, dictatorships, autocratic governments and neo-fascist movements have perpetuated conflict and propagated intolerance in several countries.

These damaged human connections have not been good for human health. Physical and mental health have suffered badly in different parts of the world, when lives have been disrupted by violence and xenophobia.

Political Divides

COVID-19 has provided worldwide evidence of how rigid ideologies and divisive political battles have created controversies and spawned disagreements on how best to respond to the pandemic. Within countries, we have seen right wing ideologues flying the flag of fake news to barricade people against science and resist masks and vaccines, not only harming themselves but also others. We have also witnessed narrow nationalism undermining global vaccine equity and obstructing scientific collaboration.

Even as the virus demonstrated how flimsy national boundaries are, incapable of stopping its spread by decree, the need for social solidarity within and across countries was not appreciated with the seriousness it demanded. Without earnest commitment to a common goal, the response was neither collective nor cohesive. It undoubtedly cost lives. Even sharing of data was not timely or complete in many cases, while conspiracy theories were advanced even by heads of nations. A confused humanity could not provide a coordinated response.

A serious political divide has also affected the global response to climate change. Even as countries waver on how speedily they will act to mitigate global warming, they are even unable to demonstrate solidarity in supporting measures for adaptation. Several low- and middle-income countries will be seriously affected by global warming, with serious health threats to their populations.[16] Support will be needed to enable them to strengthen health systems, while switching to heat-resilient and less water-intense crops.

The future of humankind depends on solidarity. Discrimination that strains human connections and hate that snaps them will harm the health of individuals and populations everywhere. All forms of discrimination are inconsistent with a civilized society that seeks to advance the physical and mental health as well as well-being of people everywhere.

The Commercial Determinants
of Health

'People are fed by the food industry, which pays no attention to health ... and are treated by the health industry, which pays no attention to food.'[1]

—WENDELL BERRY

Health gets endangered across societies when products such as tobacco, alcohol, ultra-processed foods and sugar-sweetened beverages are aggressively marketed resulting in their increased consumption. Apart from their direct effects on health, they are often accompanied by the displacement of health-promoting products either by replacement of foods consumed or by loss of income drained by addictions. Commercial determinants are associated with the production and promotion of products that negatively impact the health of people who consume them.

According to a popular definition, commercial determinants of health are 'strategies and practices used by the private sector to promote products and choices that are detrimental to health'.[2]

This identifies the private sector as the sole promoter of unhealthy practices. While substantially true, the role of the state-owned tobacco industry, the public sector profiteering from unregulated alcohol sales and dogged defence of fossil fuels by governments that derive revenue from their use and export slip through such a definition. Moreover, a product like drinking water is not detrimental to health but if a business grabs large supplies and bottles it for a price, limiting the access to free or inexpensive supply of potable tap water, then the commercial capture of even a healthy product may prove detrimental to the population's health.

Leaving aside these nuances, there is sufficient strength in the definition of commercial determinants of health to focus on the damage that private commerce has done to health over the past century. This is likely to escalate over the next century unless corrective measures are speedily employed to curb and reverse the risk to health posed by these forces. It is also true that many of these industries are environmentally harmful, exploitative of the poor and unethically target the populous markets of low- and middle-income countries.

Tobacco

Tobacco is an obvious case study of how an industry aggressively pushed a dangerous product into the lives of people, only to lead them to a den of diseases ending in death for many entrapped into the habit. Tobacco, in many forms, is an advertised addiction and a marketed malady. Over the years, the tobacco industry has promoted a variety of products, despite the knowledge of their harm to health and used devious tactics to deter, delay, dilute and derail regulatory measures.

The industry co-opted policymakers in many countries, muffled media voices with lucrative advertisements (direct or surrogate) and targeted critics with an arsenal of intimidatory threats. The stepwise pattern of rigid resistance to regulation consisted of denial of evidence, advocating freedom of choice, proclaiming the indispensable importance of tobacco to national economies (tax revenue and employment) and sponsorship of social, sporting and cultural events that purchase goodwill and lift the pressure for regulatory control (apart from serving as a channel for surrogate advertising).

These strategies have made the tobacco industry a continuing threat to global health. Recent estimates put the annual death toll due to tobacco consumption at 8.2 million (7 million due to direct 'active' consumption and 1.2 million due to 'passive' second-hand exposure).[3] About half of the regular users of tobacco die of diseases caused by it. Of them, half die in middle age.

Even the economic benefits from tobacco are illusory. The costs of healthcare and lost productivity imposed by the many diseases caused by tobacco far exceed the revenue contributed by tobacco by any estimate. While heart, blood vessel and lung diseases and a variety of cancers are the leading causes of death and disability due to tobacco, many other disorders ranging from cataracts to diabetes and infertility to impotence are now associated with the increased risk linked to tobacco.

The recognition of the health, economic, social and environmental costs of tobacco, as well as the outrage evoked by the harm to innocents caused by second-hand smoke and the repugnance towards the industry's efforts to bury the evidence of harm, led to the Framework Convention on Tobacco Control (FCTC) in 2003. This global public health treaty, developed under the auspices of the WHO and adopted to date by 182 countries, calls for several measures to create a tobacco-free society.[4,5]

Measures adopted by many countries now include increasing taxes on tobacco; ban on all forms of tobacco advertising, promotion and sponsorship; ban on smoking in public places, public transport and indoor work, dining, sporting and entertainment places; warning labels (often pictorial) on tobacco product packages; ban on sale to and by minors and support for tobacco cessation.

Alcohol

Though 'social drinking' is widely perceived to be a convivial pastime and an enjoyable accompaniment to meals in many cultures, the harmful effects of alcohol place it high among the causes of ill health and death in the global burden of disease estimates. While low levels of alcohol consumption are generally compatible with health, immoderate drinking is common and levels of tolerance vary from person to person. Women tolerate alcohol less well than men and the effects on men too vary depending on what, when and how much they drink and what they do after consuming alcohol.

It is estimated that alcohol was responsible for 3.3 million deaths per year, accounting for 5.3 per cent of all global deaths. It has been linked to more than 200 diseases and injury conditions. The young are especially vulnerable, with 13.5 per cent of deaths in the 20–39-year age group attributed to alcohol.[6] These are frequently due to accidents related to drunk driving or other risk-prone behaviours.

Alcohol damages both physical and mental health. It causes liver damage, gastrointestinal and other cancers, high blood pressure, paralytic stroke, heart failure and rhythm abnormalities, inflammation of pancreas and poor pregnancy outcomes. It disturbs mental health and opens the road to suicide. It provokes aggressive behaviour and is a cause of aggravated domestic violence. A variety of injuries, suffered by self or others, are associated with alcohol consumption. Illicit brews often contain poisons like methyl alcohol and lead to mass deaths.

Despite these facts, alcohol is a thriving global trade, with governments thriving on taxes generated from it. The alcohol industry too adopts the tactics of the tobacco industry to evade regulation, though it is less under the scrutiny of public health agencies and the media. Though direct advertisements are banned in many countries, surrogate advertising and sponsorship offer an easy path to product promotion.

Ultra-processed Foods and Sugary Drinks

Beginning in the middle of the twentieth century, the world has seen rising rates of overweight and obesity, heart and blood vessel disease, strokes or paralytic brain attacks, diabetes, cancers and irritable bowel syndrome. This period has also seen a marked rise in the consumption of ultra-processed foods. Research has shown that these two trends are associated, not by chance but by a causal relationship.

Ultra-processed foods are those whose composition has been altered by chemical, rather than mechanical, processing. This is done by the addition of a variety of chemicals. The purpose is to both enhance taste and preserve the product for a longer period.[7] Traditionally additives like salt and sugar have been used for this purpose and still are. The advent of trans-fats, involving partial hydrogenation of fats through industrial techniques, increased the scope and scale of manufacturing ultra-processed foods. Whether it is excess salt, sugar or trans-fats, all additives that are used to lengthen the shelf life of foods seem to shorten human life.

Sugar-sweetened beverages (SSBs) are also a major contributor to excess calories. They, and many of the ultra-processed foods that are rich in 'empty calories' (calorie dense but nutrient-poor), qualify for the term 'junk foods'.[8] Fructose corn syrup has been added to many such foods, pumping in calories but not nutrients. Ultra-processed foods are also shorn of several essential nutrients, especially fibre and vitamins, during processing. Manufacturers may seek to supplement these later through added fibre and vitamins but that may not restore the right balance of the nutrients present in the natural foods.

Attempts to get the manufacturers of food products to reduce the content of harmful additives and produce healthier products have not been uniformly successful. Much of the industry response has been evasive. The intent of the food and beverage industry's offer of voluntary cooperation with health agencies has been mostly pre-emptive rather than proactive towards avoiding regulation rather than actively moving for change.

Health-conscious consumer demand has brought forth some healthier food products but aggressive marketing of unhealthy products to less-aware groups continues in all countries. Some countries have adopted regulations and mandated food labelling, while others have raised taxes on sugary drinks and junk foods. However, much of the global food trade is dominated by ultra-processed foods and beverages.

Unlike the tobacco industry whose fadeout is essential and without lasting harm to society, the food industry is a part of society we cannot do without. So, the solution is to transform it to reduce its harmful potential and reshape its priorities to produce more health-friendly products. Some sections of the industry claim that it is their intent to alter their product portfolio towards that direction but the process is slow because of consumer taste preferences for the salt-, sugar- or fat-loaded foods.

Is this genuine or a mere excuse? Probably a bit of both, since the industry finds it easy to offer that alibi while conditioned tastes do take some time to change. So, the change process has to overcome both the 'credibility gap' of industry intent and the 'edibility gap' of consumer acceptance. However, taste is reconditioned in a few weeks to some months and consumer acceptance of healthier modified products will grow over time, especially if the reductions are graduated to facilitate reconditioning. So, it is up to the industry and the regulators to walk the talk.

Personal Choice?

Whether it is tobacco, alcohol or food and sugary drinks, the usual industry response is to wave the libertarian flag of 'personal choice'. It is the right of the consumers, they say, to opt for what they want and an intrusion by a 'nanny state' is unwarranted. Regulation is opposed as a matter of avowed principle because it suits the industry's interests to avoid restraint.

However, 'choice' does not occur in a vacuum. Choice is conscious, conditioned or constrained. Choice when based on correct or incorrect information access leads to the decision to consume or avoid. So, it is the duty of the collective society, especially of the government and the media, to communicate the correct scientific information as objectively interpreted by credible experts. Health and nutrition literacy of the population can influence correct choices by individuals.

Choice is also conditioned by aggressive advertising and promotional campaigns of the industry, which relentlessly bombard the consumer with the imagery of pleasurable consumption in congenial surroundings. The products, harmful as they are, become alluring and aspirational. Choice can also be conditioned by peer pressure or by cultural traditions. Smoking and alcohol consumption among teenagers is so often initiated by peer pressure, which in turn would have gathered force from advertising by the industry and its clever use of movies and the entertainment industry for product promotion.

Smoking of the 'hookah' or 'shisha' (water pipe tobacco) has moved on from a cultural tradition in some rural parts of South and West Asia to an urban youth fetish in many parts of the world.[9] Such conditioning of choice needs to be effectively countered through a combination of regulation and health education.

Even if nutrition literacy is promoted and the industry's promotion of unhealthy products is curbed by regulation, a major factor-steering choice will be the affordability of foods. If fruit, vegetables, nuts, healthy edible oils and fish are too expensive for a common family's budget, perforce the consumption will be of the less healthy products. It is a paradox of modernity that while people were previously paid for doing physical work, they have to pay for undertaking physical activity in gyms or sports venues.

Community recreational spaces are getting restricted and pedestrian pathways are getting constricted in cities. Transport too is mechanized. Under these conditions of lowered physical activity, commercial marketing of unhealthy food products assumes even more dangerous dimensions.

Moulding the Market

Unless many of the commercial determinants are modified, freedom of consumer choice remains an illusory concept. The interests of commerce are buttressed by international trade agreements that compel nations to import unhealthy products or give the industry the power to insinuate itself into free trade agreements through 'investor–state dispute settlement' provisions that are later used to sue governments that seek to restrict unhealthy products.

The tale of turkey tails exported to the Pacific Island of Samoa illustrates the coercive power of trade agreements. The USA annually consumes a huge amount of turkey meat, especially at traditional festivals, but the tails (73 per cent fat) are never eaten. This 'waste' has been exported over some decades, since the Second World War, to Pacific Island Nations. This and other ultra-processed foods displaced the traditional fibre and cereal-rich diets.

In 2007 Samoa tried to ban this unhealthy product whose consumption had grown to become a serious health hazard to its people. However, the World Trade Organization ruled against the action calling it a restrictive trade practice. Samoa and other Pacific Islands have also been flooded with fatty 'mutton flaps' (sheep bellies) offloaded by Australia and New Zealand. In 2013, obesity was prevalent in 53 per cent of men and 77 per cent of women in Samoa. Diabetes was prevalent in 20 per cent of the adults.[10]

The tobacco industry too has used the opportunities provided by free trade agreements to sue countries like Uruguay and Australia over tobacco control regulations related to tobacco product packaging, health warnings and advertising. The trans-national nature of the ownership and operations of tobacco, alcohol and food industries gives them an opportunity to seek the support of trade agreements to combat national public health measures.

The 'market' has become the reigning deity in the global economy. Nevertheless, the market is not an autonomous entity that can operate independent of, or inimical to, societal interests. It cannot remain impervious to public health concerns and unmindful of public health goals. The market has to be moulded by several forces operating in unison. They include consumer consciousness shaping the demand for healthy products; broader private sector recognition that it can benefit from the health dividend that an illness-free and productive population brings to the economy through favourable labour and consumer market dynamics; national policies that combine higher taxes and stricter regulation of unhealthy products with fiscal subsidies and supported supply chain for healthier products; international public health treaties and trade agreements that stimulate and support countries for adopting measures that can protect health from corporate misconduct and promote commercial determinants that advocate health and nutrition.

Commercial Determinants and the Environment

It is not just human health that these commercial determinants threaten. They also threaten the environment, through their processes and products. Environmental damage strikes back at human health in many ways. So, the commercial determinants are accelerating damage to health through direct and indirect pathways.

Tobacco harms the environment in many ways. The crop is water- and pesticide-intensive, apart from diverting millions of arable land from nutrient crops. Flue 'curing' requires the burning of wood. The paper used for wrapping tobacco in individual cigarettes and then packing them together for marketing fells many trees each day. It has been estimated that for every 100 cigarettes smoked anywhere, a tree has been killed somewhere. Then, the cigarette butts add heaps to environmental waste. Forest fires are frequently set off by smokers through discarded matches or glowing butts.

Another perspective, not often discussed, is that tobacco-related diseases are responsible for large hospitals being set up, which generate a high volume of greenhouse gases and have high energy consumption. Since a high proportion of hospital beds and procedures are used for the many patients who suffer from a multitude of tobacco-related diseases, it has been argued that tobacco contributes to environmental damage even through the healthcare facilities that it necessitates.

Commercial agriculture and the food industry encourage mono-cropping, reduce food diversity and use huge areas of deforested land for palm oil, corn and soya production. Ultra-processed foods also extract environmental costs all along their supply chain, including packaging and harmful food additives. Even the long transport channels of industrially manufactured ultra-processed foods and beverages extract a high environmental cost of energy use and carbon emissions.

The environmental costs of animal breeding for human consumption and water use for energy-rich but nutrient-poor beverages are very high. While the world cannot any longer depend only on local food production, like our pastoral forefathers, the hyper-commercialization of food production and marketing is not compatible with environmental stability and sustainability.

PART IV

Health System Is More than a Repair Shop

'Healthcare is vital to all of us some of the time, but public health is vital to all of us all of the time."

—C. Everett Koop

---

* Details available at https://quotefancy.com/quote/1278671/C-Everett-Koop-Health-care-is-vital-to-all-of-us-some-of-the-time-but-public-health-is

PART IV

Universal Health Coverage

'Universal health coverage is the single most powerful concept that public health has to offer.'[1]

—Margaret Chan

Should anyone's access to needed healthcare depend on that person's ability to pay for it? Is there a right to healthcare that is universal? Does it extend to all forms of healthcare or only for some? If a person does not pay out of pocket for healthcare services, then who does? How do countries set up systems to provide healthcare services to all?

Recognizing the Need for Universal Health Coverage (UHC)

The idea of universal health coverage springs from the recognition that health is both an individual need and a societal resource. Protecting the health of any member of society is a common moral obligation as well as a sound economic sense that acknowledges

121

individual health as a common productive resource for society. Social solidarity and economic investment are essential to reap the benefits of UHC, which extend to individuals, families, countries and global development.

However, formal recognition of the need for UHC, by national governments, commenced less than 150 years ago and a global movement for UHC gathered strength only in the past two decades. For most of human history, healthcare was provided to individuals by healers or doctors as a personal arrangement and organized state-funded healthcare services were available, if at all, to armies. For the indigent, charitable institutions provided some support. The poor often had no access to any type of healthcare.

Towards the end of the nineteenth century, Chancellor Otto von Bismarck of Prussia (Germany) initiated a social health insurance programme for workers.[2] This was in response to unrest among the labour unions. It also attempted to respond to the stinging social critique of reformers like Rudolf Virchow[3] who linked ill health among individuals to economic inequalities and lack of democracy in the society. Ensuring the health and productivity of the German working class was also essential for the emerging industrial revolution and for the militaristic ambitions of the Prussian empire. These convergent interests laid the foundations of a welfare state, in which health insurance was an important feature.

The Bismarck model was later adopted by the welfare states of Europe, while socialist countries in different continents aimed to provide free government-funded healthcare, as the twentieth century led to the alignment of political ideologies to the provision of healthcare as a shared societal responsibility. The Beveridge report (1942) paved the way for the establishment of the National Health Service in the United Kingdom.[4] Several other countries followed the path of UHC later, using different models to achieve the same objective. Still, much of the world was far from UHC.

The call for UHC gathered strength as the twenty-first century dawned. In 2005, the World Health Assembly of WHO adopted a resolution calling for UHC. Financing models for delivering UHC were discussed in WHO's World Health Report of 2010. The Sustainable Development Goals adopted by all members of the United Nations in 2015 clearly list UHC as a target to be attained by 2030.[5]

This target calls on all nations to 'achieve universal health coverage including financial risk protection, access to quality essential healthcare services and access to safe, effective, quality and affordable essential medicines and vaccines for all'.[6]

WHO defines UHC as a state when 'all people receive the quality health services they need without suffering financial hardship'. Different models exist for achieving this objective but universal access, assured quality and financial protection are the common features of health service provision. Health promotion, disease prevention, diagnostic services, treatments, rehabilitation and palliative care are all included in the range of services to be provided.

Progressing towards UHC

Can any country provide all of these services to all of its people, as soon as the principle of UHC is adopted? What does freedom from financial hardship mean in UHC terms? The answer to these questions was provided by WHO in the pictorial form of the UHC Cube, which has three dimensions that enclose the UHC programme space.

One dimension is 'population coverage' that represents the proportion of the people covered under any component of the UHC programme. The second dimension is 'service coverage' that represents the range of healthcare services covered by the UHC package at any given time. The third dimension is the 'cost coverage' that represents the proportion of the healthcare cost covered by the programme, to reduce out-of-pocket health expenditure and related financial hardship. Particular emphasis is laid on reducing poverty created by healthcare expenditure, while also observing limits on how much the UHC programme can fund.

The scope of the UHC programme is conditioned by the resources available at any time. Politicians will pay greater attention to the extent of population coverage, as they like to please more people (read voters) and also may pay attention to equity as a guiding principle. Healthcare professionals (read doctors) prefer a large service package that includes even expensive treatments since they believe their patients deserve the best of what science and technology can offer.

The economists and civil servants responsible for financial planning and fund allocations pay attention to the extent to which out-of-pocket expenditure can be reduced and healthcare-related poverty reduced while maintaining fiscal prudence to see that the budget is within the limits that resources permit. There is a dynamic tension between these three perspectives at any given level of resources. The resultant UHC plan must try to integrate all three perspectives to best use the available resources.

Resources are finite and cannot deliver all of UHC at once. So, the best possible package of services must be provided at each stage of its evolution, keeping both the priority health needs of the population, the potential impact of different services on reducing the disease burden and the ability of different sections of the people to pay. UHC is seen as an evolving process in every country, with changing health needs, additionally available resources and accumulating experience of programme delivery. The general consensus is to aim for 'Progressive Universalization'.[7, 8]

The need for staged realization of UHC led to advocacy for its being labelled at the start as 'pro-poor' universalization, with the targeting of the poor to begin with. While well intended, this advocacy did not take into account the fact that many 'targeted' programmes intended for the poor turned out to be poor in design and delivery. That is because the more influential sections of the society, the middle class and the affluent, had no stake in its success.

Even if it is appropriate to preferentially address the health needs of the poor, that preference must be embedded in a system that serves all and binds all to its success. Hence, the term 'progressive universalization' denotes both a staged expansion and a prioritization of the poor at each stage so that health inequities are minimized as UHC evolves.[9]

Choosing between Options

How do we make choices, from among the various healthcare options, at any stage of UHC? Cost-effectiveness is an indicator that favours one service modality over another. It answers the question 'how much more health can we achieve for the money invested?'. Since financial protection and poverty reduction are important objectives of UHC, health economists are also recommending an 'extended cost-effectiveness analysis' that tags another question 'how much of financial protection will be provided by including this component in the package?'.

By using this criterion, costly tests or treatments that are essential will not be excluded, as they not only add to health but also protect from financial shocks from high out-of-pocket expenditure.

Besides cost-effectiveness, equity too must be a strong consideration. Otherwise, some lifesaving therapies for rare disorders may be excluded and the health needs of vulnerable sections may be ignored. If lifesaving surgery for a child with a congenital heart defect or chemotherapy for childhood leukaemia is entirely dependent on the parents' ability to pay, many sick children will die. If society deems it a broader custodial duty to rescue a child from child neglect or domestic violence, then is medical treatment too not a societal responsibility? So, equity must lie at the heart of UHC.

In the context of UHC, equity may be viewed in two dimensions. Horizontal equity ensures that all persons are entitled to the same services, without discrimination. However, that alone will not bridge the health gaps created by cumulative inequalities that some sections of the population have experienced earlier. Some of these inequalities have an inter-generational effect too. So, the programme must also incorporate mechanisms to promote 'vertical' equity that direct additional resources or services to the groups whose health indicators are much behind others. Tribal and urban slum populations in India are an example.

Financing UHC

How will UHC be financed? How will it reduce the financial burden on individuals, while utilizing the funds efficiently to maximize health gains? These questions have been addressed differently by different countries. For the answer to these questions, we need to understand the concepts of risk pooling, purchaser, provider and service package.

UHC operates on the insurance principle of risk pooling, even when it does not employ a contributory health insurance model. When a large number of people constitute a risk pool, only some of them get sick at any given year. Their healthcare expenditure will most often exceed the premium paid by or for them. However, this will be subsidized by the many other contributors who are not sick at all or have minor illnesses that year. The healthy subsidize the sick at any time, though the composition of those who get sick will vary within the group across time.

Usually, the young cross-subsidize the elderly, as they fall ill less frequently. When they grow old, they too will benefit from the protection afforded by risk pooling. Tax-funded health systems constitute the largest risk pool since the whole population is covered. In them, the rich cross-subsidize the poor since they usually pay more direct taxes than the poor. It is not as though the poor do not pay taxes. They do, through indirect taxes that are levied on the goods they buy as necessities, such as soap or clothes.

The purchaser of services from the healthcare providers is either the person (out of payment) or an agency that pays on the person's behalf. In UHC, the objective is to minimize the person's out-of-pocket expenditure. So, the government pays from tax revenues or the insurance company pays from the risk pool fund of paid premiums or an employer pays on behalf of an employee, directly or through an insurance company. So tax revenues, employer-funded insurance and privately purchased insurance are the main channels of healthcare financing.

There is an advantage of pooling all or many of these funds into a single-payer mechanism. That ensures a large risk pool. It can help expand the service package. It also gives the purchaser the power to negotiate prices and set quality standards when dealing with many service providers from a position of strength. That is the power of a monopsony where a single purchaser can buy from any of several competing providers. It is the converse of a monopoly, where a single provider holds power over multiple purchasers.

Even if purchasers of private insurance do not opt for a single-payer system, governments and employers who pay for UHC service coverage to their beneficiaries will gain an advantage through a single-payer system operated by an autonomous agency established by the government.

Providing and Paying for Services

The providers will vary by sector (public, private, voluntary), level of care (primary, secondary, tertiary) and discipline. They may be part of small or large institutions or be solo practitioners. The informal healthcare providers who are not professionally qualified and practitioners of traditional systems of medicine do not usually come into this group but some countries may include caregivers formally trained in traditional medical systems.

The modality of payment is very important. The conventional practice, prevalent in many countries is for anyone seeking healthcare to be billed for each visit, test, procedure or hospitalization episode. This is the 'fee for service model'.[10] However, this creates a perverse incentive for the healthcare provider to order more review visits, tests, procedures and hospital admissions than are needed. An alternative model is the 'capitation fee model',[11] where the healthcare provider is paid a fixed amount annually to provide all the needed healthcare to a person during that period. These costs may exceed the paid sum for an individual who has serious or prolonged sickness that year. However, these individuals will be few in number compared to the total number registered with the provider under this scheme. So, the principle of cross-subsidization works.

There is also an incentive for the provider to focus on health promotion, disease prevention and risk factor control to avoid the costs of costly advanced care. Such an arrangement works best when there is a network connecting providers in primary, secondary and tertiary care. Such an arrangement is called 'managed care with capitation mode of payment'. There will be an incentive to limit the costs at the advanced care end of the spectrum by focusing on preventive and primary care.

If blood pressure and diabetes are well controlled, the need for costly coronary bypass surgery or renal dialysis and transplantation can be avoided. To avoid 'rationing of care' through avoidance of referral for advanced care, the adoption of standard management guidelines and periodic technical audits will help check the perverse incentive for cost-cutting in this method.

UHC is both a moral imperative and an economic incentive for protecting the health of all individuals who comprise the population of any country. It is also one of the best symbols of social solidarity. As we advance our civilization in the twenty-first century, UHC needs to reflect the collective commitment of all nations to move 'health for all' from an aspirational agenda to an accomplished reality.[12]

Our Healthcare Needs Other People Too

'To know even one life has breathed easier because you have lived. This is to have succeeded.'[1]

—RALPH WALDO EMERSON

Will there ever be a time when a person can go through his or her entire life, from birth to death, with all healthcare needs being met only by robots primed by artificial intelligence, without having to seek help from even one other human being? This may happen in overhyped projections of a technology-driven future that we see in science fiction or tech industry predictions, but extremely unlikely to occur in the foreseeable future.

It is difficult to envision a time when a person will never need a fellow human being as a doctor, nurse, radiology technician, physiotherapist, vaccinator, mental health counsellor or organ donor. Some humans also will be developing drugs and vaccines that are needed for people they may never meet. So, a person's healthcare too is *connected* to others!

A Healthcare Workforce

When people are involved in the delivery of healthcare services, through an organized health system, we call them collectively the healthcare workforce. Individual healers have existed from ancient times, practising myriad methods and known by diverse names in different lands. Organized systems of traditional medicine evolved over time. Many of them saw the functioning of the human body as being shaped by its relationship with nature. Even as spiritualism was invoked as a healing power, harmony with nature was considered essential. Ayurveda, in India, embodies this philosophy that continues to this day. This is also true of many other ancient systems of medicine.

Over time, traditional systems of medicine evolved from individual healers to organized systems with schools of training. From learning by apprenticeship to collegiate education was a big leap that modern medicine brought. Strong foundations of scientific methods, with laboratory-based training, were demanded by reforms ushered in the early twentieth century.

The Flexner report (1910),[2] the Welch-Rose report (1915) and the Weir report (1932) ushered changes in medical, public health and nursing education, respectively. We then saw a global profusion of medical colleges and nursing schools, though public health schools had a slower growth. COVID-19 is now providing a growth spurt to public health schools.

Allied health professional training too gained scale and has sped up over the past six decades. Medical and laboratory technicians, physician and surgical assistants, radiographers, physiotherapists, rehabilitation professionals, optometrists and mental health counsellors are among the many categories of allied health professionals who are much needed and are being trained, not to mention dieticians and yoga teachers. Healthcare became a team function, rather than a limited interaction between a single healer or doctor and the patient.

Shortage of Healthcare Providers

Despite the rapid growth of organized medicine and nursing, the world is witnessing huge shortages in the healthcare workforce across the world. The WHO estimates a shortfall of 18 million healthcare workers by 2030.[3] This is likely to be an underestimate, as advancing non-communicable diseases and mental health disorders will require skilled healthcare workers to provide chronic, continuous care. Shortages will be experienced all over the world but will be especially severe in low- and middle-income countries (LMICs). High-income countries (HICs) have ageing populations with low or negative population growth. This depletes fresh recruitment into the healthcare workforce, even as retirements continue. The LMICs lack investment for scaling up training institutions and lose a large number of those trained because of migration to HICs as the latter offer better pay and working conditions.

Even within the scenario of an overall global shortage, there are huge global inequities. Among WHO's six global regions, Africa (with 24 per cent of the global disease burden) has 3 per cent of the global healthcare workforce. In contrast, the regional grouping of the Americas (with 10 per cent of the global disease burden) has 37 per cent of the global healthcare workforce. It has been estimated that Africa would need a minimum of 6000 additional healthcare workers by 2030.[4]

In keeping with an expanding list of global healthcare priorities, WHO revised its estimates for the number of healthcare workers needed per 10,000 population. In the context of the Millennium Development Goals of 2000 (MDGs), a minimum of 22.8 healthcare workers (doctors, nurses and midwives) was considered the norm for such a population unit. However, the MDGs only targeted maternal and child health and three major infectious diseases. Now the WHO estimates that a country would need 44.5 doctors, nurses and midwives per 10,000 population[5] to achieve the more numerous health targets linked to the Sustainable Development Goals (SDGs). This is especially true of universal health coverage (UHC). Many countries of the world fall short of that.

India, for example, has 22.5 doctors, nurses and midwives per 10,000 population. This is about half of WHO's norm.[6] However, when we exclude self-reported doctors and nurses who do not have proper qualifications and those who are not in active service in their professions or are not in the country, the number shrinks to 4.8 doctors and 5.7 nurses per 10,000 population. In contrast, a large number of India-trained doctors and nurses are actively serving in the USA, UK and Gulf countries.

While new medical and nursing colleges are being set up in India, there are huge regional disparities within the country, in terms of both the number of training institutions and the number of healthcare personnel available. Within each region too, there are marked urban–rural disparities, with two-thirds of the healthcare workforce located in urban areas that only account for one-third of the population.[7]

Technologies can enhance the skill sets of healthcare workers, bridge some of the access gaps and enable better connectivity across different levels of care. However, they cannot substitute a multi-layered, multi-skilled healthcare force needed by a well-functioning health system. Trained healthcare workers will be needed in higher numbers and better distributed within and across countries, even as health technologies are employed for their skill enhancement. Improved effectiveness and reduced costs of healthcare will come from the appropriate use of health technologies but they will not find impactful utilization in the absence of an adequate healthcare workforce, which is available and able to use them.

Filling the Gaps

Deficiencies in the number and skills of healthcare workers in LMICs will not only impact those countries adversely. Weak disease surveillance and management systems in developing countries will result in infectious diseases spreading across the globe. High disease burdens, which reduce the life expectancy and productivity of working-age populations in LMICs, will not only destabilize labour and consumer markets in those countries but also have adverse effects on a globalized economy that operates on international investments and supply chains. Depleting even the limited healthcare workforce of LMICs by drawing them to HICs will not do the world any good.

The challenge of meeting the whole world's healthcare workforce, adequately and equitably, needs global solidarity and co-investment. HICs can provide financial and technical support to LMICs for training and skilling large number of healthcare workers, to take advantage of the large populations and younger age profiles. Only a small and pre-defined proportion of those trained with such assistance may be declared eligible for international migration to the financing country. Ideally, migration should not exceed that limit. Even if migration is considered an individual right and not subject to quotas and restraints, the developed country that is receiving a trained healthcare professional from a developing country should accept an obligation to compensate both for the cost of training and for the opportunity cost.

Simultaneously, financial and technical assistance should also improve healthcare infrastructure and equipment in LMICs, so that the push factor of poor working conditions can be mitigated. Countries can also work together to set up a global emergency task force that can be quickly assembled and moved to regions experiencing a public health emergency.

Such arrangements call for global solidarity. Unless politicians and people appreciate the interconnectivity of global health challenges and the interdependence of countries in finding regional and global solutions, we will continue to see the world weakened by unabashed and uncompensated poaching of healthcare workers, refusal to share technologies except at high profit and politically expedient espousal of narrow-minded nationalism.

We are indeed one world and we need to share our resources in providing needed healthcare services for all persons in all countries. Both good sense and good values demand that we create and support a global healthcare workforce that cares for all of humanity.

Health Promotion Needs Social Policies

'Promotion of health generally by improving the standard of living. From the health point of view, we are in this connexion first and foremost interested in the three fundamental environmental factors: housing (including family life), nutrition and working conditions (including human relations as well as material conditions).'[1]

—KARL EVANG

Health is not merely the absence of disease or infirmity, says the WHO. It defines health as a state of 'complete physical, mental and social well-being'. While most people would agree with this description, some health experts like Fallon and Karlawish[2] argue that it is unrealistic and also incorrect to require a 'complete' state of physical well-being for saying a person is healthy. They point out that many persons with well-controlled hypertension or diabetes do experience a high level of well-being.

I agree with this view. Many persons may have sub-clinical disease and feel healthy till symptoms show up or the disease is detected on some screening test. If we insist on complete physical well-being, we will end up branding most elderly persons as unhealthy and deny active and happily independent persons with a physical disability the feeling that they are leading healthy lives. Indeed, everyone can gain from improved societal conditions and personal practices that can enhance the physical, mental or social dimensions of their health at any stage of life. This will translate into a health promotion across the life course.

The health of persons is shaped and altered, across their whole lifetime, by many factors. While some factors may be more dominant than others, at different points in time, it is the interplay of these varied influences, which determines how healthy or ill we are and how well or unwell we feel at any given time. Health promotion programmes aim to steer those influences in a positive direction and remove barriers on the road to health and well-being.

Health Promotion Gets an Identity

While early notions of health promotion focused almost exclusively on personal behaviours and placed the onus on individuals to cultivate and practice them, a broader framework emerged in the Ottawa Charter.[3] This visionary document, adopted at the first international conference on health promotion (1986), incorporated five action areas: build healthy public policy, create supportive environments for health, strengthen community action for health, develop personal skills and re-orient health services.

The importance of the social and environmental determinants of health was long recognized by eastern systems of medicine and by public health champions who emerged in Europe. However, the system of modern medicine grew increasingly tethered to a biomedical framework that ignored the non-biological influences and interactions. The Lalonde Report (1974)[4] of Canada was the

first western government report that sought to liberate health
from such a restrictive paradigm. It emphasized the need for the
prevention of health problems and the promotion of good health as
important priorities besides the healthcare system that responds to
the needs of those who become sick. This report gave a fillip to the
health promotion movement.

While recognizing the many determinants of health, the aim of
all initiatives in health promotion is to assure good health at the
individual level. There has been great emphasis on behavioural
change among individuals, whether it is the adoption of, and
adherence to, practices that protect and improve health or the
giving up of habits and behaviours that harm health. From giving
up addiction to smoking or alcohol to becoming physically active
and eating more plant-based foods, efforts were made to change
knowledge, attitude and practice (the much talked of KAP) through
behaviour change communication (BCC).

While factors operating at the individual level are undoubtedly
important, there are many societal factors that can enable or impede
behaviour change. It has been well recognized that knowledge alone
does not change behaviours, especially when habits are well set or
addictions have taken a firm grip. It is possible to use knowledge
effectively to get people to consider the positive or negative outcomes
of behaviours but to get them to act with purpose and commitment
to change, much more is often needed.

What Is Needed?

To change set behaviours, a person should be able to say:

1. *I understand the need to change.* This requires knowledge that
   the person is provided by others or finds by themselves.

2. *I wish to change.* This calls for motivation, generated by self or through inspiration.

3. *I have the ability to change.* This requires the skills needed to make change happen.

4. *It is possible to change if I try.* This comes from the recognition that there is no social or environmental factor preventing change or making it very difficult.

5. *Support is available to help me change.* These can be in the form of social support systems or healthcare services.

There are many models of behaviour change developed by social scientists. Ultimately, the process of behaviour change involves an interplay between personal, social and environmental factors. Here, I include economic and commercial determinants under the broader label of social determinants. In some areas, it may be mostly the individual factors that propel or impede change. In others, it may be the social milieu or the physical environment that may drive or obstruct change.

The objective of health promotion has to be to enhance the personal capabilities of individuals to protect, preserve and promote their physical and mental faculties that represent a healthy state while acting upon on an array of societal structures and functions to align them to the objectives of population health.

Enhancing Health Literacy

The health literacy of individuals has to be enhanced, for enabling them to make the right choices and volitionally initiate change. This has been traditionally done through mass media, local community influencers, peer groups or family members. In the era of mobile phone suffusion and social media surge, digital channels have become most influential. Unlike in the past, where much of the messaging was done through personal interactions or impersonal mass media, the social media interaction is both distant and personally engaging.

While it can be educational, conveying correct information in a concise and crisp manner, it can also be the purveyor of misinformation and a propagator of fake news. It is necessary to ensure that correct information is crisply conveyed to capture attention and convince the recipient that behaviour change is needed and would be beneficial. Reinforcement helps but needs to be refreshingly innovative and not boringly repetitive.

Strengthening Motivation

Motivation to adopt health-promoting behaviours usually comes from the benefits one perceives for oneself, either from anticipated gains in health and wellness or from harm reduction expected by giving up deleterious practices. Physical activity, for example, offers the reward of better body shape, fitness, stress reduction, a greater sense of wellness and improvements in blood pressure and blood sugar levels. Motivation comes from the knowledge that some or all of these benefits will accrue from adopting moderate physical activity as a regular practice.

Social approval for adopting the new behaviour and appreciation for the results achieved are great motivators. Practicing healthy behaviours alongside others can be a great motivator too, like jogging or practicing Tai Chi in groups. Peer influence has been known to be an effective motivator. Guidance from an expert can overcome diffidence. Having a good instructor for yoga can be a strong motivator.

Motivation can come not only from enlightened self-interest but also from ennobling altruism. Smokers may give up that harmful addiction not only to reduce the personal risk of dangerous diseases but also when they wish to avoid harming others (especially close family members) through second-hand smoke. People may reduce meat consumption to not only protect their health but also protect the planet by reducing greenhouse gas emissions from livestock. Safe driving is practiced to not only avoid personal injury but also avoid causing trauma or death to others.

Developing Skills

Behaviour change needs skills that can be acquired through self-directed learning, using resources available in print and electronic media, or developed through training provided by others. Either way, the learner is dependent on guidance from others. Parents teach us how to brush our teeth correctly, teachers at school tell us about how to differentiate between healthy and unhealthy foods, driving school instructors teach us safe driving, public health experts teach young people how to firmly say 'no' to tobacco when subjected to peer pressure and support groups tell addicts how to give up alcohol, drugs, tobacco and other harmful addictions.

We learn through observation, training, trials, practice and re-skilling. Whether it is individual learning or group learning, the skills needed for successfully practicing health-promoting behaviours are acquired through our social connectivity.

Many government health departments and community-based voluntary organizations employ trained health promotion specialists who work with communities, to not only impart knowledge and motivate people but also assist in skill development. However, many others can do it too, from parents and teachers to peers and media influencers. Think of the Jane Fonda workout videos, the many bestselling yoga training books and videos or the many healthy eating cookbooks. We can gain skills, if we are motivated to change and wish to learn. Again, others in society play a role.

An Enabling Environment

Even when a motivated person has acquired the knowledge and skills needed to adopt a health-promoting behaviour, social and environmental circumstances may pose barriers that thwart those attempts. Society must adopt policies that remove or lower those barriers, so that it becomes easier to initiate and sustain behaviour change. Policies can also 'nudge' individuals and groups to overcome hesitancy to initiate and earnestly pursue behaviour change.

Policies can be highly impactful in changing people's behaviours even if they are non-personal in their nature. Fiscal instruments like higher taxes on harmful products (tobacco, unhealthy food products and sugar-sweetened beverages) not only reduce consumption by raising prices, but the extra revenue that initially flows into the exchequer can be used for promoting health literacy and enhancing services for universal health coverage.

Even if these taxes are not earmarked for health, the expanded revenue pool will permit higher allocations to the health budget. To reduce the impact of higher taxes on the poor, the revenue may be spent preferably on welfare programmes that benefit them. Subsidizing healthier food products, especially in the public distribution system, will make healthy foods more affordable.

Benefits from a healthy public policy have an inter-generational carryover of benefits. Creating clean public spaces, which have low levels of air pollution and are free of tobacco smoke, will reduce health risks for those born in the future, apart from promoting the health of the present generation. As will agricultural policies and food systems that leave a legacy of dietary diversity with balanced nutrition, while restoring commitment to environmental sustainability.

Replacing urban chaos with habitable and equitable housing and safer mass transport systems will not only reduce health risks now but also protect health in the future. Protected pedestrian pathways and safe cycling lanes can provide protection against road accidents and promote physical activity across multiple generations.

Policy interventions to promote health cost much less than healthcare interventions to diagnose and treat diseases. So, they are cost-saving. Measures like raised taxes can actually raise money for the government to spend on welfare measures. Several of the benefits accrue soon so that 'discounting' of future benefits by economists does not affect their monetary benefit. When the quality of life is measured and included in the analysis, the benefits appear larger and even more immediate.

While policy measures are useful as 'nudge' instruments to stimulate behaviour change and 'enabling' instruments for removing barriers to health-promoting practices, such policy measures will require public support. Promoting health, nutrition and environmental literacy among people will generate a popular demand for beneficial policies and mobilize citizen support for their introduction and implementation. A virtuous cycle can be created, of policies fostering better health among people and they, in turn, demand even more policy changes to further benefit health.

As people start practicing health-promoting behaviours, they may need assistance for gaining more information, clarifying doubts, reinforcing motivation, correcting relapses to unhealthy behaviours, or connecting to peer groups. A number of voluntary groups help to support people to reach their goals in areas such as de-addiction, weight loss, physical activity and mental health.

Quite often support comes from family members, friends and peer groups who can share experiential wisdom and help in locating resources that may be needed for skill enhancement or overcoming barriers.

Health Promotion Needs Social Relationships

A well-publicized Harvard Study[5] followed men for 80 years to study what affects their health. The Harvard Study of Adult Development found that people's relationships and how happy they are in those relationships have a profound influence on their physical and mental health. Close and happy relationships were better predictors of long and happy lives than genes, IQ or social class. 'Tending to your body is important, but tending to your relationships is a form of self-care too' was the conclusion that the study's director Robert Waldinger drew from the study.

While the goals and rewards of health promotion are customized to serve the aspirations of health and well-being at the individual level, the various elements of health promotion depend on people's connectedness for their success. From gaining awareness and information to finding motivation and support, other people are involved.

Policy measures are not tailored for individuals but impact many lives. It is this tapestry of human connections across communities of people that enables individual persons to promote their health and well-being. As Barbara Streisand sang in the film *Funny Girl*, 'People, people who need people, are the luckiest people in the world'.

On the Wings of Science and Technology

'The glory of medicine is that it is constantly moving forward, that there is always more to learn. The ills of today do not cloud the horizon of tomorrow, but act as a spur to greater effort.'[1]

—WILLIAM JAMES MAYO

How much did we, as human species, gain in life expectancy in the past 120 years? The answer will astonish persons who do not research these facts as part of their academic pursuits. The world average of human life expectancy was 31–32 years in 1900. In 2019–20 it was 72.6–73.2 years.[2] Even though COVID-19 impacted that trajectory since 2020, the 230 per cent rise in life expectancy is a remarkable achievement. There are considerable disparities within and between countries, which need to be recognized and redressed. However, we have undoubtedly done very well as a species.

How did this happen? There are two major contributing factors, both related to civilizational advance. Social conditions vastly improved in terms of water, sanitation, hygiene, housing, nutrition, education, women's empowerment, decolonization, greater respect for human rights and economic security supported by social safety nets.

At the same time, there have been remarkable scientific advances that have given us profound insights into the intricate biology of the human body and its many maladies as well as the ability to apply correctives through highly impactful technologies and behavioural interventions.

COVID-19 and the Strength of Science

The COVID-19 pandemic not only brought forth the follies of human-aided zoonotic viral transmission but also catalysed the amazing speed and skill of the scientific response. From genomic analyses of the virus and its fast-growing brood of variants to vaccines that were developed in record time, science displayed its dazzling array of talents. Lifesaving drugs emerged from fast-paced adaptive clinical trials and tele-health services were being offered to patients managed at home even as intensive care units offered support to lungs ravaged by the virus.

Other than COVID-19 too, there have been many miracles of modern science that have overcome disease and averted death. From organ transplantation to implantable cardiac defibrillators and gene therapies to stem cells, the list is long and never short of wonderment at what human intellect and ingenuity can achieve. Machine learning and artificial intelligence have energized digital health, even as robots entered surgical theatres to operate on patients who may be later monitored through wearables.

Barriers to Beneficial Use

However, the dizzying speed with which technologies have emerged should not blind us to the pitfalls of techno-addiction that may misguide the choice and use of technological tools. Obsession with seeking technological solutions for health problems ignores the many determinants of health and forgoes the opportunity to use impactful non-technological solutions. Ignoring the need to strengthen the health system has also impeded the delivery of impactful innovation, resulting in a technology pileup whereby the products do not reach the intended beneficiaries.

Gaping inequities also separate those who can access and afford innovative technologies from those who are barred by patent and price barriers. Overuse of and inability to use health technologies are two aberrations that detract from their value, distort the application of science and diminish its contribution to human health. Health systems driven by the profit motive of healthcare providers overuse expensive technologies, such as imaging scans and unnecessary surgeries or stents, despite the increase in financial and even biological costs to the patients. On the other hand, poorly resourced health systems are unable to provide lifesaving technologies to many who need them.

One of the paradoxes of the global COVID-19 vaccine supply has been the fact that African populations in whom the clinical trials were conducted were among those who had the least access to them. This is more the norm than an exception, even in the case of drug trials conducted in low- and middle-income countries.

Perils of Proprietary Science

Inequities, within and across countries, are also exacerbated when patent protection prevents widespread manufacturing of impactful, even lifesaving, technologies. Even when gravely threatened by a global pandemic like COVID-19, vaccine manufacturers have been extremely protective of patent rights and reluctant to share knowledge with others who can contribute to the global response. Even prior to this pandemic, the pharmaceutical industry invoked patent rights, attempted 'ever-greening' to keep patents alive even after their expiry and demanded data exclusivity. When the world was reeling under the impact of the HIV-AIDS pandemic, a leading multi-national drug company found it fit to litigate against South Africa for importing lifesaving drugs at low cost from an intrepid Indian generic manufacturer.[3] Imagine the effrontery of suing Nelson Mandela's government that was strenuously trying to save lives as AIDS was devastating Africa!

When the Doha declaration of the World Trade Organization[4] eased patent restrictions for public health emergencies and lifesaving medical interventions, commercial interests attempted to outflank it by inserting provisions for Investor-State Dispute Settlement (ISDS)[5] into free trade agreements between countries. The WTO is a forum for settling disagreements and disputes between countries, represented by governments. By introducing ISDS into the free trade agreements, commercial interests represented by the industry can insert themselves into the process and attempt to stall public health measures. The tobacco industry has tried to do that by litigating against countries that were introducing tobacco-control measures. This provision has been invoked in many areas, from the price of privatized water supply to cities to the price of medicines to counter public health measures.

Innovation merits rewards by way of societal recognition. Some monetary rewards too may be given as incentives. However, it should not be the overriding objective creating barriers to societal benefit. While affirming that 'ideas fuel the economy', a respected British journal *The Economist* editorially declared that 'today's patent systems are a rotten way of rewarding them' (August 8, 2015).[6] It argued that the unimpeded sharing of information and ideas stimulates fresh innovation. The vast talent of the human collective can advance science and technology faster and for greater social benefit, if there is a free flow of ideas and a ready exchange of experience. There have been suggestions that Innovation Prizes be awarded for breakthrough scientific achievements but not restrict wider access to the knowledge or products.

If it is argued that much monetary and intellectual investment goes into scientific innovations, requiring profits both as compensation and as further investment into the new scientific enterprise, it can be countered through two other facts. First, much of the foundational science that underlies scientific innovations are supported by publicly funded research grants. Often, even clinical trials and product development are supported by government grants. Second, low- and middle-income countries contributed much wealth to their colonizers for the development of scientific institutions and many migrating scientists in the post-colonial era. Both economic and intellectual property were boosted in high-income countries, while they were depleted from the low- and middle-income countries. If reparations were demanded for these, where will the defence of patent protection stand? Eschewing any such polemical exchanges, the global solidarity demands the pooling of economic and intellectual resources across the world for advancing the common good and combating the common threat.

Proprietary science is an impediment to progress. If climate change is a threat to the whole planet, should access to green technologies be the preserve of only a few countries? Is it conscionable that access to vaccines in a pandemic period be contingent on patent holders asking national governments to pledge their sovereign assets? Science is sterile if it does not serve a social purpose. In the twenty-first century, that social purpose is global good—for all of humanity.

Need for Team Science

The widely propagated image of a solitary scientist coming up with mind-boggling discoveries and miraculous technologies is true only to a very limited extent. Even if such a discovery is made, the scientist will need the wider world to know, applaud, adopt and apply. However, most scientific endeavours need several researchers working as a team. Often combining several disciplines. Solutions to complex problems require many minds and several skills to solve. Subsequent application too needs many persons to open and operate channels for impactful implementation.

When the world celebrates 100 years of the discovery of insulin in 2022, it would do well to remember that it was a collaborative effort of Banting, Best, Macleod, Collip and other colleagues.[7] The discovery transformed the treatment of diabetes. Incidentally, Banting refused to put his name on a patent, as he felt it was unethical to profit from a discovery that can save lives. Collip and Best sold the insulin patent to the University of Toronto for a mere $1 (one dollar) because they wanted all of humanity to benefit from the discovery.[8]

As science advances, we are becoming increasingly aware that the biology of health, health systems and social determinants of health are a multi-verse of complex adaptive systems that interact with and influence each other. The purpose of health research is to provide evidence-informed, context-relevant, resource-optimizing, situationally adaptable, culturally compatible and equity-promoting recommendations for policy and practice. This requires a confluence of basic, epidemiological, clinical, management, social and behavioural sciences along with health economics and health technologies. Science, with all its purity, must contend with the real-world political economy of health. It is, therefore, essential that research becomes collaborative and capable of crossing disciplinary boundaries to connect scientists who can overcome complexity to advance human health and well-being.

Overcoming Fake Science and Anti-science

Since ancient times, science has encountered sceptics and even violent opponents. Giardano Bruno was even burnt at the stake for his cosmological theories that in the modern era might have won him a Nobel prize. Many others have faced fierce critics within the scientific community itself. Some scientists, like Lysenko, persecuted other scientists for challenging views before being discredited.[9] Even well-meaning scientists are not infallible in their observations and deductions.

However, science has shown the power of self-correction, after some time even if not immediately.

It is the emergence of large anti-science movements, often allied with extreme right-wing politics and religious obscurantism, that has been a retrograde feature of the twenty-first century. Denial of the COVID-19 pandemic, violent protests against face mask protection and refusal to accept vaccines have flown in the face of scientific evidence. Conspiracy theories abounded as trust in scientists diminished. The commercialization of science led to suspicion even about sound scientific advice. Trust deficit proved to be a much bigger enemy of public health than in the twentieth century.

At the same time, fake science too held sway. Confident assertions were made about effective treatments, either with no data or fudged data. Undue emphasis on the publication numbers of researchers, impacting their career progression and research grants, provided a perverse incentive to publish fraudulent reports even in prestigious peer-reviewed journals. When exposed, they would lead to retractions. Fake science also became a weapon for anti-science groups to counter sound science. Commercial interests, like tobacco and fossil fuel industries, promoted their own brands of industry-sponsored research to deny tobacco-related health harm or global warming due to climate change.

To weed out fake science and vanquish anti-science, saner sections of humanity need to unite and strive together to assert the power of rational thought over the forces that seek to sap the strength of science while misusing the technological products of science for their mission. The ability of anti-science agitators and fake news purveyors to use the internet to spread lies is a strange illustration of how scientific advances can be used to hurt science itself.

Moving Ahead

It is essential that all persons who share the belief that science should be utilized for the benefit of all humanity must unite to protect the potential of science to promote, preserve and restore human health. It requires believers in science and practitioners of science to act in concert, all across the world. Without global solidarity, science will be forced to fly only with one wing. It will make the journey to better health neither swift nor safe. We need to connect to properly harness the power of science and the potential of technologies. The future of global health depends on that connectedness.

PART V

Environment Is Our Life Support

'Man is the only animal that fouls its own nest.'

—ANONYMOUS

Progress Should Not Impose
Pollution Penalty on Health

'Pollution should never be the price of prosperity.'[1]

—AL GORE

'Our natures are the physicians of our diseases.'[2]

—HIPPOCRATES

Planet Earth supports life, unlike many others that our scientists have identified and investigated through sophisticated techniques. Our planet provides us the air, water and soil that can sustain life. And not only human life but also many other forms of life that range from unicellular organisms to advanced forms of multi-cellular plants and animals of many species. These natural resources helped to create life and enabled billions of humans to lead healthy lives over many millennia. Yet, we take them for granted and seldom pay attention to their quality with the same level of interest that we take in the appearance of our bodies and the concerns we have about the quality of healthcare we receive from hospitals when we fall sick. The indifference is costing us heavily as we are actively

155

or passively contributing to the pollution of these life-sustaining natural resources. The consequences of that drift will be disastrous for human health.

Recognition of the relationship between our physical environment and human health is not new. Thousands of years ago, Hippocrates cautioned travellers that they must be mindful of the quality of air and water in the places that they intend to visit, as it would affect their health. He disputed the prevalent notions of diseases being caused by evil spirits and emphasized the role of climate as a major determinant of health. The relationship of climate and environment to the biological processes of living organisms is now recognized in the burgeoning science of 'bioclimatology'. This is vital to an understanding of human health—both of individuals and of the social collective they belong to.

Air Pollution

The major pollutants of air are particulate matter, ozone, nitrogen oxides, carbon monoxide and sulphur dioxide. Particulate is the pollutant most frequently referred to in the media and measured in air quality reports. The other pollutants too need to be measured for a comprehensive assessment of air quality, as they too have health effects.

Particulate matter is usually reported in the sizes of 2.5 microns (PM2.5) and 10 microns (PM10). Just to have an idea of how small these are, compare them to single human hair (50–70 microns) and a grain of sand (90 microns).[3] PM2.5 group comprises combustion particles, organic compounds, metals, etc. PM10 assortment has dust, pollen and mould among its constituents. Ultrafine particles are of a much smaller size (0.1 microns or less).[4] As aerosols, they can enter the lungs and penetrate deep into the distant regions of the lung where the air sacs (alveoli) are located in abundance.

As gas exchange takes place in between the air in the alveoli and the smallest blood vessels (capillaries), these particles can also enter the bloodstream. Besides damaging the lung tissue, they can also endanger many other organs where they are deposited by the bloodstream.

Sources of particulate matter are vehicles (line sources), power plants and factories (point sources), dump sites and sewage treatment plants (area sources), forest fires and volcanoes (natural sources). Atmospheric aerosols are formed from vehicular emissions, biomass burning, industrial emissions, wind-blown dust and volcanic emissions. Biomass burning is common in many poor households of South Asia and Africa where cooking gas and electricity are not easily available for use in kitchens. Open-fire cooking produces smoke comprising fine particles, carbon monoxide, polycyclic aromatic hydrocarbons, dioxins and pesticide residues. This smoke is the kitchen's curse for the women who cook, the babes in their arms and the toddlers who play around their mothers.

The WHO estimates that 7 million deaths occur each year due to air pollution, as over 90 per cent of the world population lives in areas that do not meet WHO's air quality standards.[5] Exposure to air pollution results in acute and chronic respiratory disease, coronary heart disease (heart attacks), strokes (brain attacks leading to paralysis), lung cancer, high blood pressure, diabetes, obesity, cataracts, neonatal deaths and dementia. Black carbon nanoparticles derived from combustion have been found in human placentae and in the frontal cortex of brains in autopsy samples. When mothers are exposed to air pollution during pregnancy, there is an increased risk of pre-term birth, low birth weight, height deficit and poorer mental development in children. It is tragic when scientists report that the brains of children exposed to heavy air pollution in Mexico show features similar to that of Alzheimer's disease.[6]

Air pollution produces extensive inflammation in the lungs, blood vessels and many other body tissues. Acute and chronic respiratory diseases, cardiovascular disease, diabetes and obesity are manifestations of systemic inflammation. Even during the COVID-19 pandemic, regions that had higher levels of air pollution had higher rates of mortality from the disease compared to areas with better air quality within the same country. Even the risk of tuberculosis rises with exposure to air pollution. Depression, anxiety, dementia and suicidal tendencies have also been noted to have a higher risk associated with poor air quality.

WHO recently revised air quality standards, lowering the thresholds from earlier recommendations. This is because a growing body of research evidence shows that harm to health from air pollution occurs well below the previous cut-off values. Indeed, the risk of damage to body tissues and disease occurs across a rising slope of risk, rather than across fixed thresholds. The revised guidelines of 2021 recommend 24-hour and annual average level thresholds for PM10, PM2.5, ozone, nitrogen dioxide, sulphur dioxide and carbon monoxide, with lower limits than were set 15 years ago.[7] The world now needs to implement policies to ensure that these thresholds are not breached, by placing a premium on human health.

Water and Soil Pollution

Water is polluted through biological and chemical contaminants, with many adverse health effects. When water sources are contaminated with human or animal excreta, pathogenic microbes proliferate and cause severe diseases such as diarrhoea, amoebic dysentery, giardiasis, cholera, typhoid, hepatitis, meningitis, polio and toxoplasmosis. Unclean water for washing can cause skin and eye diseases, through microbial contaminants.

Sewage contamination of water sources is a landmark case in the history of public health. In 1854, John Snow investigated an outbreak of cholera in London and traced it to the contamination of the water supply from a sewage line in Broad Street.[8] Removing the handle of the water pump there ended the outbreak. Despite great advances in public health engineering since then, sewage is still allowed to mix with water supply in different parts of the world. In rural areas, the bathing of cattle in rivers and ponds allows their excreta to mix with water where cooking utensils are cleaned or clothes are washed. This is because a clean water supply is not available to all households.

In cities of both developed and developing countries, callous discharge of sewage into water sources has been reported even recently. Southern Water, a privatized water company in the UK, was fined £90 million in July 2021 for deliberately dumping billions of litres of raw sewage into protected seas near Kent and Hampshire over several years.[9] The pollution contaminated shellfish from it are consumed by humans. Southern Water pleaded guilty to 51 counts of knowingly permitting contamination of coastal waters with untreated sewage. This was done to avoid the costs of sewage treatment.

Chemical contamination of water occurs because of industrial effluents being discharged into rivers, lakes and other waterbodies. Rivers in India have shown the presence of pharmaceutical effluents, including antibiotics. When such effluents from firms manufacturing pharmaceutical products are allowed to flow into public water sources, many adverse health effects can occur in exposed humans and animals. When pharmaceutical wastewater is released into soil and water, breeding sites are created for drug-resistant bacteria. Of 283 bacterial isolates of *E. Coli* from River Cauvery in southern India, all were resistant to third-generation cephalosporin.[10] Similar were the reports from River Musi in Hyderabad.

Minamata disease is a severe neurological disorder described in Japan in 1956.[11] It was related to methylmercury poisoning that occurred in humans who consumed contaminated fish and shellfish. A factory had discharged inorganic mercury into Minamata Bay. The toxicity of human exposure to mercury became widely recognized thereafter in many countries, with toxic effects on the nervous system, kidneys, blood and bone marrow becoming clear. Recognition of these effects led to the international Minamata Convention of 2013,[12] which resolved to control the anthropogenic release of mercury throughout its life cycle. If we do not find mercury thermometers and blood pressure measuring instruments with mercury columns in use today, it is a result of the awareness of mercury toxicity that came from Minamata.

Other Forms of Chemical Pollution

Thomas Midgley was a famous American chemist of the twentieth century. Working with General Motors, he introduced two industrial innovations that were widely adopted and acclaimed but were later decried as major threats to the environment and human health.[13] One was the development of chlorofluorocarbons (CFCs) as non-inflammable refrigerants. CFCs became notorious later for punching holes in the atmospheric ozone layer and have been banned. Before CFCs, Midgley invented leaded gasoline for car engines, as an anti-knock fuel. The health hazards of lead exposure became widely known later, leading to a ban. In both cases, the industry denied mounting evidence of harm till the huge mass of irrefutable scientific facts forced regulatory action to ban the products.

Lead toxicity came from leaded petrol, lead-acid batteries and leaded paints. In children, it resulted in cognitive deficits, attention deficits, behavioural problems, poor academic performance, aggression, violence, crime, reduced physical growth, hearing loss, dental caries and delayed sexual maturation. In adults, it caused kidney dysfunction, hypertension, cardiovascular disease, peripheral neuropathy and central nervous system damage, reproductive dysfunction and effects on pregnancy and lactation. Lead is also excreted in breast milk, harming the baby's body and brain.

The world took several years to recognize the health hazards of dichlorodiphenyltrichloroethylene (DDT), used widely the world over as an insecticide before its ban. It is now slow to impose regulatory controls on a horde of endocrine-disrupting chemicals (EDC). These are naturally occurring or manmade chemicals that mimic or interfere with hormonal function in the body. Many EDCs bind to body fat, have long half-lives and bio-accumulate. They are called persistent organic pollutants (POPs). EDCs include pesticides like DDT, chlorpyrifos, glyphosate and atrazine. They also include phthalates, bisphenol A, lead and cadmium. These are used in children's products, personal care products, food contact materials and medical tubing. POPs include brominated flame retardants, polychlorinated biphenyls (PCBs) used in electronics and building materials and dioxins produced from burning plastic.

Exposure to EDCs affects several body systems. Reproductive system effects include reduced fertility, abnormalities in male reproductive organs, early puberty in females, pre-term delivery and birth defects. There is an increased risk of cancers of the breast, ovary and prostate. Children manifest neuro-developmental defects. Metabolic effects include the development of diabetes, obesity and metabolic syndrome. The immune system is affected, with an increased risk of asthma and allergic disorders.

Chemical pollution also manifests as pesticide residues in food. Fruits, vegetables and grains are routinely sprayed with pesticides. When there is a high level of exposure to these pesticides, there is strong evidence of adverse health effects such as cancers, diabetes, asthma and neurological disorders. Farmers and their family members have been affected. Studies in India have shown a high prevalence of diabetes among farmers exposed to organophosphates. It was observed that the gut microbiome is affected by the pesticide setting in motion a cascade of metabolic changes that induce glucose intolerance through gluconeogenesis. A study in the USA showed that while consumption of low pesticide residue in fruits and vegetables (4 servings per day) reduced the risk of coronary (ischaemic) heart disease by 20 per cent, no such protection was found when the fruits and vegetables had a high pesticide residue.

Arsenic is another chemical that accumulates in rice, much more than in other crops. Even when drinking water is arsenic-free, rice intake contributes to arsenic exposure in adults and children. Global warming increases arsenic levels in rice. Long-term exposure to arsenic through drinking water or food increases the risk of skin disorders, diabetes, high blood pressure and several types of cancer.

Plastics as Pollutants

Plastics are non-biodegradable and slowly break down into microplastics. They contain harmful chemicals such as bisphenol A (BPA) and phthalates. Styrofoam contains cancer-causing chemicals such as styrene and benzene. Microplastics are particles of plastic materials, which are less than 5 mm in diameter. They are primarily produced for commercial use in personal care products, plastic pellets and clothing. Microfibres are shed from such clothing. Secondary microplastics are formed from the breakdown of larger plastics such as water bottles.

Chemicals in plastics act as endocrine disruptors, affecting the body's hormonal balance. BPA, for example, mimics oestrogen. Animal experiments have consistently reported toxic effects that span a wide spectrum of reproductive, immune, genetic and nervous system abnormalities. The burning of plastics produces dioxins and furans that are carcinogenic. Styrene and benzene in Styrofoam are cancer-causing chemicals. Littering and dumping of plastics lead to blockage of sewage and drainage systems which in turn cause flooding, mosquito breeding and transmission of vector-borne diseases. Plastic pollution of lakes, rivers and seas is endangering aquatic life, disrupting marine ecosystems and disrupting the environment.

Why Is Pollution Control So Difficult?

With such profusion of scientific knowledge about the harmful effects of pollution, why is the control of pollutants making such slow progress across the world? It is because polluting industries and other commercial entities that are the sources of pollution, or are the agents of their dissemination, fiercely fight regulation. They first deny the evidence, then manoeuvre to delay, dilute and derail regulatory measures. Governments too are often slow and soft in their responses, daunted or even co-opted by the financial might of the polluters. It is easy to pick on the person who throws a candy wrapper on the street but when it comes to the fossil fuel industry, the pesticide industry or the automobile industry, governments prefer to plead rather than penalize. Ordinary citizens learn to silently suffer as they get on with their mundane lives. In permitting pollution to continue its assault on people's health, we will passively perpetuate its grip on humanity. The generation that will soon be born will enter a highly polluted world, not of their making.

If we recognize and respond to this threat, collectively as a society, we can change the dynamics of policymaking and the patterns of corporate conduct. For that to happen, each of us must recognize that our health is being affected by forces that others control and that it is necessary for those who wish to change the sorry status quo to unite—to design, dictate and deliver the alternate agenda of development. So, the change-makers of the world, young and old, must connect to decisively dispel the pall of pollution that hangs over human health.

Do Humans Trigger Zoonotic Pandemics?

'Ecological circumstance provides the opportunity for spillover. Evolution seizes the opportunity, explores the possibilities, and helps to convert spillovers to pandemics.'[1]

—DAVID QUAMMEN

COVID-19 opened up a huge debate on its origins. The WHO is still investigating whether the SARS-CoV-2 virus originated through a spillover across species in a wet market in Wuhan or the result of an accidental lab leak. Either way, the virus was first identified in samples of bat faeces isolated from caves near Wuhan. The transmission across species occurred thereafter, whether directly to humans or through an intermediate host like the pangolin that landed in the wet market as an exotic food favoured by some people. This is, by all counts, a zoonotic pandemic.

Such zoonotic outbreaks have become recurring features over the past six decades. They may be limited outbreaks within a country, spread across a region or become truly global by reaching the danger level of a pandemic. Like an intermittent fever that spikes at intervals, media coverage of infectious diseases rises to a high pitch whenever a new killer outbreak is reported anywhere in the world. The fear of global spread alarms the general public and keeps public health agencies on high alert.

Zoonotic Infections Have Grown in Frequency and Spread

This has been true in recent years even before COVID-19, with SARS, H5N1, H1N1, MERS, Ebola, Zika, and Nipah viruses becoming familiar names in the rogues' gallery of viruses that move from animals to humans. The interval between these spikes has been shortening over the past six decades, even as the media's speed in spreading scary news has increased markedly. So, it feels as though we are under siege most of the time, with viral marauders reported regularly across our highly connected world.

A rational response to such outbreaks requires an understanding of why these viruses cross species, how they are transmitted among humans, what preventive measures can be taken, which tests and treatments exist and whether the health system is ready to contain the outbreak at an early stage.

Initiation of Zoonotic Spillovers

Joshua Lederberg, who was awarded the Nobel Prize for his discoveries in bacterial genetics, wrote that an axiomatic starting point for further progress is the simple recognition that humans, animals, plants and microbes are co-habitants of the planet.[2] Instabilities arise in this dynamic relationship because of ecological and evolutionary causes. A pandemic arises when there is serious instability, allowing the virus to reach humans through an ecological breach. Over time, an equilibrium point is reached where the virus coexists by becoming less virulent but retaining or even increasing its infectivity. Evolutionary biology guides such a change in the virus so that it does not decimate its limited host, lest its own species gets extinguished. While this is a desirable outcome, much damage can be done if the virus reaches pandemic proportions before it simmers down.

Zoonotic diseases (transmitted from animals to humans) account for over 60 per cent of infectious outbreaks.[3] Deforestation due to expanding agriculture and logging, animal breeding and livestock farming is creating a conveyor belt for the transmission of microbes, hitherto confined to their primary animal hosts in wildlife, to the veterinary population and then to human habitats. Anthropogenic climate change creates conditions for vectors like mosquitoes and ticks to spread to new geographies. They transport the microbes to the human body. Man, thus, falls victim to his own ecological follies. Bats did not choose to live amongst us—we forced them to become part of our expanding habitat.

Evolutionary Biology Drives Microbial Mutations

Evolutionary forces then take over. Microbial genetics evolve far more rapidly than humans. Microbes that are confined to forest animals or small human communities follow the survival rules of evolution, and generally have low virulence because the extinction of their host will lead to their own extinction. However, humans now crowd together in large numbers, travel fast and far in many modes of transport and unknowingly transmit microbes to other humans through sputum, saliva, semen, blood and other bodily fluids.

This enables the virus to multiply rapidly and mutate to more virulent forms. Even if it kills over half of those it infects, there is still a large host population remaining to ensure its own survival and propagation. In general, highly transmissible strains (like H1N1) are not highly virulent and highly virulent strains (like H5N1) are not highly transmissible. However, these dynamics depend on how large and easily accessible to the virus the susceptible host population is.

So, the seesaw of survival maintains a balance between microbes and humans. However, microbes must be vigilantly monitored during outbreaks to study if highly infective viruses are suddenly seized with mutation madness to develop higher virulence, especially in crowded populations where the virus has a free run. Such mutations can occur because of 'antigenic drift'[4] or 'antigenic shift'.[5] The former happens when the mutation is within the genetic material of the virus itself. The latter involves the exchange of genetic material with another type of virus. The latter can spell danger if the exchange takes place with a more virulent type of virus.

An Ecological Response Is Needed

The response to the zoonotic outbreaks, which impose high health, economic and social costs on humans cannot lie only in vaccines, medicines and masks or in lockdowns, travel bans and xenophobia. Humans must recognize that the best defence lies in respecting natural boundaries and not obliterating the protective barriers that lie between the microbes that reside in the forest and humans who lead lives in urban or rural congregations beyond the forest.

Does this mean forests are out of bounds for humans? Not so. For thousands of years, several indigenous (tribal) communities have lived close to or even in the forests. However, they respected the laws of nature and lived in harmony with the rest of forest life. They did not kill animals for sport but only in limited quantities for food. They did not have vast tracts of forest land, forcing forest-dwelling microbes to seek new hosts among veterinary or human populations. It is the respectful connectivity with nature that enabled the co-existence with other life forms. In turn, forests yielded medicines for healing and nourishing nutrients through a variety of wild plant foods. Trekking in the forests can be an adventure sport that humans can enjoy, but deforestation comes with huge penalties for climate change and zoonotic outbreaks that can turn into pandemics.

Even as we must advance science to study the nature of microbes and develop defences against those of them that pose danger, we must respect ecological sanctity to avoid the dangers of spillover in the first place. For that, we must recognize that the health of humans is connected to other life forms in a delicate ecological balance that we must respect.

Even 'Lab Leaks' Are Due to Human Errors

The vast majority of the zoonotic pandemics are due to 'natural origins', resulting from spillover of a virus that is present in nature from one species to another. However, the origin of the COVID-19 pandemic has been clouded by a controversy about the virus having possibly leaked from a laboratory in Wuhan where 'gain of function' studies were being conducted. Such studies seek to create mutations in a naturally sourced virus (in this case from bat droppings in caves near Wuhan), to study if infectivity, virulence or immune evasion can be enhanced. The ostensible reason is to prepare for possible mutations with effective vaccines and drugs. But that is a dangerous game. If the highest standards of bio-security are not maintained, the mutant virus can escape from the laboratory to trigger a pandemic. Even if such standards are maintained, scientists cannot prevent misuse by autocratic despots, military dictators or dangerous terrorists for biological warfare. The whole world can be endangered if biosecurity is breached accidentally or intentionally. Neither legitimate curiosity nor arrogant vanity of scientists should give sanction to such research.

Loss of Biodiversity Harms
Human Health

'Every morsel of food, every sip of water, the air we breathe is the result of work done by other species. Nature gives us everything we need to survive. Without them, there is no us.'[1]

—ENRIC SALA

As individual life forms on earth evolved over time, the nature of their interdependence too evolved. However, humans allowed their sense of superiority over other life forms to endanger many of them and drive several to extinction. A report in 2018 estimated that while humans constitute only 0.01 per cent of all living things by mass, they have caused the loss of 83 per cent of all wild animals and half of all plants on this planet.[2] By damaging and depleting biodiversity, we not only disrupt the intricate balance of nature but also deny ourselves the many direct and indirect benefits that accrue from our ability to link and learn from other life forms.

Healthy Nutrition Requires Dietary Diversity

A healthy diet requires a balance of several nutrients drawn from a variety of food sources. Most of them are derived from plants. Even animal foods that humans consume draw on plants as the initial source of nutrients that those animals used for their nourishment. These plant sources of animal nourishment range from grasses and leaves to marine plankton. The large array of grains, fruits, vegetables and nuts that humans consume is the gift of a rich natural biodiversity of the plant kingdom. In addition to cultivated plants, wild plants yield a variety of fruits, such as berries. An animal-mediated product like honey is mostly sourced from the wild where bees feed on plant pollen. An array of edible and medicinal oils exists in wild plants.

Even the staples in our diet reflect shrinking biodiversity. In Asia, the varieties of cultivated rice have fallen to just a few dozen from several thousand that reflected a rich biodiversity not so long ago. Biodiversity builds soil health, even from decaying plants and animals, and in turn nourishes plant and animal health that benefit from soil nutrients. Isn't it strange that humans who like to pick from a variety of foods from a menu card in a restaurant are increasingly limiting the range of foods that can nourish the soil? The very soil that serves an abundance of life forms, including us humans.

Biodiversity Loss and Climate Change Harm Each Other

One of the commonest causes of global warming is the loss of the earth's green cover. Deforestation strips that protective cover. Along with that, it also destroys many pollinator species that help new plants to spring. Of the many animals and birds that are among these pollinators, bees are the most energetic in assisting plants to reproduce. Habitat loss, pesticide use and global warming are endangering several species of bees. If they dwindle and disappear, we will not only lose the honey but also much of our foliage and fruit.

Loss of the planet's green cover causes global warming. In contrast, it has been estimated by scientists that nature-based solutions can provide up to 37 per cent of the carbon dioxide mitigation needed to counter global warming and contain the rise of the earth's temperature below a 2 per cent limit.

Biodiversity Protects Against Pests

Damage to crops from pests is a danger that farmers are concerned about, in every part of the world. The damage varies from 10–16 per cent on average, according to Biodiversity International.[3] However, sometimes the loss may be even 100 per cent in some locations in some years. Climate change is aggravating this problem. The rise in ambient temperatures carries the dual danger of insect proliferation and an increase in their appetites. A research study, published in *Science* in 2018, reported that yield loss due to global warming could lead to 10–25 per cent loss for each degree centigrade rise in temperature, for wheat, rice and maize, which are globally the most consumed staples.[4] So, a 2-degree rise in temperature could lead to 50 per cent loss due to increased pest-related damage.

Biodiversity provides protection against pests in many ways. It provides a large range of natural predators against pests, apart from being a source of natural pesticides from plants. It helps to create resistance genes and shape community-level ecology to provide local biodiversity defences against attacks by pests. Crop diversity fosters stronger defence against insect damage, while monocropping diminishes the mix of insects that provide ecosystem services.

Biodiversity Builds Resilience Against Natural Disasters

We are fast losing the protection offered by biodiversity against natural disasters like floods and storms. The loss of over 35 per cent of the earth's mangrove forests has made us vulnerable to floods and is resulting in rising sea levels that threaten coastal habitations and destroy farming. Deforestation, with the loss of multiple plant species, is damaging soil integrity and causing landslides precipitated by loose soil.

Biodiversity Supplies Medicinal Products

Medicine has greatly benefited from several plant- and animal-derived products. Several antibiotics, anti-malarial, anti-cancer drugs, anti-inflammatory medicines, heart and blood pressure drugs owe their origins to plants. Traditional medicine systems across the world have been dependent on the healing powers of herbal products. As we understand more about the role of the microbiome in guiding our health and nutrition, our appreciation of natural foods and medicines is increasing. Animal products derived from snake and scorpion venom have been used to develop anti-clotting drugs. Anti-hypertensive medicines, like captopril and enalapril, used in modern medicine, have been refined from snake venoms.[5]

Many innovations in medicine and surgery have borrowed ideas from natural designs. Scientists in Massachusetts recently used a spinach leaf's delicate veinous system to overcome a block in tissue engineering of the human heart.[6] Cellulose is a biocompatible material that has been used in bone and tissue cartilage engineering. By destroying many species, we will deprive ourselves of the benefits of the many intelligent designs perfected by nature.

Biomimicry

The amazing diversity of nature, shaped by evolution, gives us a remarkable variety of biological designs in different plants and animals. Several of the designs have inspired not only artists but also innovators in chemistry, biology, medicine, architecture, biomedical and structural engineering and technology. Since nature has not patented any of these designs, we could liberally borrow to invent new products and then patent them!

This field of biomimetics or biomimicry has given us many useful designs and products. Some of them are familiar, like the shape of aeroplanes akin to birds, fluid-drag reduction swimsuits that adapted the design of shark's skin and Velcro fasteners that were invented by George de Mestral[7] when he noted how burdock seeds clung to his socks and dog Milka. High-strength carbon nanotubes have been modelled on the unshakable adherent strength of byssi in mussels that can cling to rocks despite powerful waves sweeping across them. Legs of robots have been inspired by those of the cockroach and the micro hairs on the soles of the gecko.

While biomaterials, for use in the human body, have been derived from many materials such as metals and ceramics, scientists in Massachusetts reported in 2017[8] the use of a spinach leaf to build working heart muscle. They overcame a roadblock to tissue engineering by using the delicate veins of the leaf. They removed the plant cells to leave behind the cellulose frame of the veins and bathed the cellulose frame in live human cells to grow a mini heart.

Cellulose is a biocompatible material that has been used in bone and cartilage tissue engineering and wound healing. The remarkable potential and performance of biomaterials is impressively presented in a TED Talk by Oded Shoseyov.[9]

By destroying many species, we will not only deny ourselves the beauty of nature but also deprive ourselves of the benefit of many intelligent designs developed by nature. Biodiversity is a treasure we cannot afford to waste away, even for this reason.

Health Hazards of a Planet in Peril

'Climate change will affect the basic elements of life for people around the world—access to water, food production, health, and the environment. Hundreds of millions of people could suffer hunger, water shortages and coastal flooding as the world warms.'[1]

—NICHOLAS STERN

As sizzling summer temperatures broke records in 2018–19 and a spate of natural disasters brought a spate of floods or devastating droughts to the world in the last decade, we have been warned that the planet is perilously close to the tipping point of irreversible climate change. Even as the impassioned advocates of urgent climate action and science-denying sceptics debate the surety and speed of climate change, the adverse impacts on health and nutrition are posing a mounting menace on human survival and well-being. Unfortunately, these have not been adequately informed and understood by most of the planet's population.

'Global Harming' with Weather Vagaries

Let us start with the extreme weather conditions. We are witnessing unexpectedly severe summers and winters with a frequency that they are becoming the usual pattern. When the summer temperatures soar, people fret about global warming, but when icy winters arrive cynics sneeringly question if global warming really exists. Since both these extremes are manifestations of climate change caused by global warming, the whole phenomenon may be best understood as 'global harming'.

Both high and low temperatures harm human health since the human body can function well only within a limited temperature range that allows the body temperature to be maintained around 37 degrees Celsius (98.6 degrees Fahrenheit). The body does have adaptive mechanisms - blood vessels on the surface can dilate to expel heat or constrict to conserve it and sweat can be used as a mechanism that cools through evaporation. However, these are stretched beyond the limits of adaptation if the weather conditions are extreme; age limits the degree of body's response and pre-existing diseases increase vulnerability.

Heat exhaustion, heat stroke and circulatory failure are increasingly severe manifestations of exposure to severe heat. Persons in outdoor occupations (like agricultural workers or construction workers), playing outdoor sports or cycling to work and the homeless are especially likely to suffer severe or prolonged exposure. The elderly will suffer because the blood vessels have less elasticity and reduced ability to adapt to changes in blood volume resulting from dehydration. Even brain strokes and paralysis can result from dehydration and an increase in blood viscosity. Persons with pre-existing cardiovascular or renal disease become especially vulnerable and contribute to high death rates from extreme heat. As heat levels rise, the risk of intra-group and inter-group conflicts increases due to increased irritability, less patience and also competition for scarce water resources. It appears that people grow especially hot under the collar as the temperatures soar!

Babies have a higher content of water in their bodies (75-78 per cent) in comparison to adults (60–65 per cent) and less ability to sweat. They are, therefore, more likely to suffer from the effects of dehydration as well as a rapid rise in body temperature. They are also less resilient to severe cold. Thus, the very young, the elderly, the diseased and the poor will suffer the most because of their vulnerability, offending our civilizational commitment to protect the weak, infirm and the age groups that are most dependent on society for the protection of their health and well-being.

Extreme cold too can threaten health, with direct effects ranging from frostbite to hypothermia and indirect effects extending from depressed immunity to increased risk of heart attacks and strokes. Again, the very young, the elderly, the poor and those exposed outdoors to harsh temperatures will be the most vulnerable. Road traffic accidents, due to low visibility and skidding road conditions, also rise resulting in death or disability. Frigid winters also increase the incidence and severity of mental disorders such as depression, especially if scant sunlight results in a string of dark and gloomy days.

As nature weeps over human folly, weather events take the form of excessive rainfall or cyclones with flooding of a populated area. Severe heat can also lead to droughts resulting from the paucity of rain and forest fires triggered by excess heat. Coastal areas will be devastated by rising water levels as high temperatures heat the seas. Many coastal cities may disappear as will some island nations. These will result not just in geographical alterations on maps but manifest as terrible human tragedies with loss to life, physical injury and mental trauma. Climate refugees will add to the number of involuntary migrants, driven by floods, drought, water crises and unliveable temperatures. Persons with physical or mental disabilities will be at high risk in extreme weather events because of the reduced ability to move to safer locations.

Prolonged heat waves, frigid winters and extreme weather events causing floods or famine affect the economy at both national and household levels, through losses in productivity and property. Daily wage workers are especially vulnerable to income loss. These economic impacts will have cascading effects on the health of individuals, families and populations.

Health services too will be compromised by extreme weather events unleashed by climate change. Torrential rain, flooding and cyclones impede transport, restrict the mobility of healthcare providers, snap the supply chains of drugs and equipment and may physically damage healthcare facilities. If power failure and breakdown of protected water supply also add to this misery, lifesaving equipment such as intensive care units become non-functional and essential services cannot be maintained. From movement of ambulances on the road to the functioning of ventilators in critical care units of hospitals, the vital health services that can save lives will be severely disrupted.

Infectious Diseases Will Spread Farther and Faster and Chronic Diseases Will Corrode Health

As the heat rises, mosquitos that thrive in warm weather conditions will be able to climb to higher altitudes, displaying athletic agility in ascent even as humans grow listless in the torpid weather. Vector-borne diseases such as malaria, transmitted by mosquitos, will gain new ground. Even at lower levels, mosquito-borne diseases such as dengue and Zika will spread faster and farther as heat and humidity provide the stimulus for their vectors to multiply.[2]

As the availability of potable drinking water decreases, waterborne infections will spread through the consumption of contaminated water. Diarrhoea, especially among children, will become a killer. Bacterial, viral and parasitic agents of deadly or debilitating infections, which lurk in contaminated water, will become more widely prevalent. Hepatitis, cholera, gastroenteritis, dysentery and typhoid will become prevalent as contaminated water and unsanitary living conditions combine in the aftermath of climate-related natural disasters. Heat also enables deadly fungal infections to appear and spread, like *Candida auris*; it emerged as recently as 2009 as a killer with 60 per cent mortality among those infected.

'Bracing for Superbugs: Strengthening environmental action in the One Health response to antimicrobial resistance' is the title of a report released by the United Nations Environment Programme in February 2023. It states that climate change and antimicrobial resistance (AMR) are two of the greatest threats to the global health and are interlinked. It states that with global warming, the gradients that drive the evolution of AMR with accelerate. Inger Andersen, the UN Environment Programme's executive director says, 'The same drivers that cause environmental degradation are worsening the antimicrobial resistance problem. The impacts of antimicrobial resistance could destroy our health and food systems.'[3, 4]

As climate-related floods, famine and extreme weather create waves of climate refugees, their unsanitary living conditions will make them easy prey to infections. The infections some of them have carried with them from their native locations will spread to their new neighbours in the host population who do not have acquired resistance to the infections to which they had no prior exposure.

Chronic diseases too will become more common. Increases in heat and humidity will cause a rise in chronic respiratory diseases, aggravate asthma and disturb mental health. Cancers of the skin and lung will become more common. Heart attacks and strokes will be precipitated by prolonged exposure to heat stress and water shortage. Injuries, with resultant chronic disabilities, will also be a consequence of climate-related natural disasters.

Agriculture and Food Systems Will Be Strained and Nutrition Security Threatened

A major impact of climate change will be on agriculture and nutrition security. Crops will be affected by water stress and heat stress which impact the type, quantity and nutrient quality of the crops produced. Marine life too would be affected by rising aquatic temperatures, affecting fish stocks. Rising sea levels will increase the salinity of the freshwater sources that connect to the sea, affecting the quality of water available for agriculture and aquaculture. Natural disasters like floods and vagaries like excessive or unseasonal rainfall will damage crops.

Production of staples like wheat and rice will be reduced due to rising temperatures. In many parts of South Asia and Sub-Saharan Africa, which even presently grow these crops at the upper margin of their temperature resilience, further increase in temperature will reduce both the quantity and the quality of crop yields. It has been estimated that in these regions a further one-degree centigrade rise in temperature will reduce crop yields by 7–10 per cent.[5] Increased carbon dioxide in the atmosphere will also reduce their nutrient quality. Even the nutrient content of non-staples will be affected. Fruit will ripen early and rot early in the heat. Water-intensive crops will suffer from water shortages induced by climate change.

The Last Nail or a New Deal?

Despite the amazing leap that the human family has made in health and well-being since the emergence of the Homo Sapiens, climate change could well be the nail that seals the lid on its future. Extinction is a real possibility. Even on the road to perdition, which may be several hundreds of years away, we will see severe setbacks to the health and well-being that the human race has achieved since it learned to walk on two feet.

It behoves us all, as the most intellectually advanced species in the animal kingdom and self-elected custodians of the planet's future, to display the right combination of sensitivity and sensibility to ensure that the health and well-being of future generations are not put in peril by accelerated climate change that is clearly anthropogenic. Otherwise, we will be squandering the gift of health that nature and nurture have combined to confer on most of the humans now alive. Despite our scientific fascination with our genes and the confidence that we can manipulate them, we will be curtailing their future if we carelessly cause the damaged environment to guillotine their future. To prevent that calamity, we need to not only gaze intently into the hidden secrets of the cell but also grasp the message that comes to us from the cosmos with increasing clarity and urgency. Our genes will survive and thrive only if we take care to let our planet survive and thrive. We are not on a lonely planet, but this is our only planet!

PART VI

Creating the Future

'In weighing the fate of the earth and, with it, our own fate, we stand before a mystery, and in tampering with the earth we tamper with a mystery. We are in deep ignorance. Our ignorance should dispose us to wonder, our wonder should make us humble, our humility should inspire us to reverence and caution and our reverence and caution should lead us to act without delay to withdraw the threat we now pose to the earth and to ourselves.'

—JONATHAN SCHELL

Vision of a Healthy Society

'If we do not create the future, the present extends itself.'

—TONI MORRISON

We need to collectively envision the ideal of societal well-being and then chart a path to that destination. This vision must encompass the aspirations of individual nations and the interconnected world while extending the assurance of a healthy global society to the generations that will follow us.

A society that embraces well-being must have the strength of shared commitment of the vast majority of its population, to the development and sustainability of efficient, equitable and empathetic health systems and supportive social systems. Those systems must create equality of circumstances, by bridging existing social inequities that translate into health inequities. This they must do through action on the social determinants of health, to give an equal start to a healthy life. They must also then provide equality of opportunities for every individual to develop to the full potential across a full and fulfilling life course.

To use the capability paradigm of Amartya Sen and Martha Nussbaum,[1] a confluence of capabilities must be fostered in all individuals, without impediments from adverse social determinants. We must recognize, measure, monitor and reduce inequalities in all spheres of development that impact sustainable well-being. Only then will the individual right to health become a collective societal obligation.

As such capabilities are being developed, we should not permit well-being to be thwarted by the commercial determinants of health, which prioritize profit for a few over the public good of the many. We must ensure that the dominance of market incentives over moral imperatives does not undermine efforts to advance societal well-being. The market cannot be an autonomous entity impervious to public health concerns. From the profit-seeking push for the increased sale of tobacco products and alcohol to aggressive promotion of ultra-processed foods and sugar-sweetened beverages, many agents of ill health are advertising addictions that result in marketed maladies. The fossil fuel industry seeks to protect its profits, unmindful of the perils to humanity posed by unmitigated climate change. The menacing growth of the arms industry, protected by right-wing rhetoric on unrestricted individual freedom to bear arms and a self-proclaimed obligation to intervene in other nations in the name of global security, unleashes gun violence within countries and wars between countries.

We must make the markets sensitive and responsive to public health priorities through consumer consciousness, regulatory measures that judiciously combine incentives and disincentives, international conventions and trade agreements that protect health and the environment while promoting social justice. The private sector too must recognize that the health and well-being of society offers a growth dividend to the economy that will benefit everybody, or else the economy will keep slipping on the banana skins of successive public health failures.

For societal well-being, we need to promote a scientific temper, where multi-disciplinary evidence informs policies and practice. As we deal with many complex adaptive systems dynamically interacting with each other, we must reduce dependence on linear models of social analysis and use the knowledge gathered from several sciences and diverse sources. As Louis Pasteur advised, we must keep our enthusiasm but let strict verification be its constant companion even as we step away from conventional constructs.[2]

We must end sectarian strife and parochial prejudice that threaten the well-being of the human collective. We need to create a globally harmonious society where migration is not a trapdoor to danger and discrimination but an open gateway to new opportunities and cultural confluence. We need to foster cultural diversity, not by mere tolerance but by open-minded acceptance and open-hearted appreciation. We need to build a healthy global society on the foundations of social solidarity, within and across countries.

The present generation of young persons is living in a present dominated by the long shadow of the COVID-19 pandemic and is seeing a world riven by polarized politics, social discord, widening economic inequality, xenophobic discrimination, religious divides and anti-science movements. The future they see is of advancing climate change, economic slowdown and growing unemployment. That is not a picture of societal well-being. We need to collectively create a better alternative.

Aspirations and apprehensions of the young, about their future, must be recognized by the present generation of policymakers, decision shapers and programme implementers in diverse domains of sustainable development. Actions taken by current leaders of societal development and governance must be closely monitored by an intergenerational combination of independent observers who have no conflicts of interest. Health impact assessment and environmental assessment, of national and transnational development programmes and policy initiatives, must guide the path to health assurance that is illuminated by the values of equity and social justice.

The benefits of health promotion, at the societal level, will extend across several generations, by creating the legacy of healthy habitats, which are free of environmental pollution and tobacco smoke, while providing dietary diversity through nutrition-friendly agriculture and food systems. The growth of healthy cities must provide opportunities for safe social interaction and physical activity without destroying forests or disturbing ecological balance.

Inter-generational carriage of the benefits of health promotion is mediated through pathways that involve both epigenetic effects and social system design. Such long-term benefits are seldom estimated in a conventional economic evaluation of initiatives for health promotion. Yet, such sustained inter-generational benefits are of the greatest value for societal well-being.

We will need new models of societal governance. At the political level, we need participatory democracy—not merely representational democracy. At the health system level, we need people partnered with public health with active engagement of communities. At the administrative level, we need digitally enabled decentralized decision-making for effective programme implementation. At the global level, we need more equitable policies in global health governance, coordinated by a stronger United Nations.

While being energized by the timeline of 2030, set by the Sustainable Development Goals,[3] we must recognize that health promotion needs continued commitment to societal well-being. The arrival of 2030 will not blow the final whistle on our play for sustainable development. It will mark the half-time, as many of the health and climate change goals will continue to engage our attention at least till 2050. Unfortunately, this is a game where we will not have the play continuing into extra time if we fail to score the goals by then. So, let us pace our game well, with an eye on the ticking clock.

Recognizing this urgency, as we resolve to realize this vision, we must create coalitions for change, by adopting an Action Almanac that has several components:

- Assemble Allies
- Adopt an Agreed Agenda
- Amplify Advocacy
- Accelerate Action
- Assert Accountability

This is the path we must pursue if we have to realize our resolve to create a healthy global society that survives and thrives in a healthy planet.

What Will the Young Persons of 2051 Say?

'We enter the future backwards.'[1]

—PAUL VALERY

I am not writing this because I have any illusion that I or this book will be around in 2051. As a person born in 1951, I do not expect my life expectancy to stretch that far. Very few books have a readership beyond a couple of years after their publication and I do not nurse the vanity that this book will evade a vanishing end to endure till 2051. If it can presently stir up a discussion and spark a reaction among the young persons to whom it is addressed, it would have served its purpose.

What I am really curious about is what the young person of 2051 (perhaps born in the decade after this book was written) would say about the issues that I have written about. If perchance a copy of this long-forgotten book should accidentally surface in physical or electronic form in 2051, what would someone born in 2030 say or write about it as a comment? Incidentally, 2030 is the year when the Sustainable Development Goals (SDGs), adopted in 2015 by all member countries of the United Nations, are to be achieved. Would the SDG targets have been achieved by the year our protagonist of the future is born? 2050 is the year by which most countries should have fulfilled their pledged commitments to slow down global warming, made at COP 26 (held in Glasgow in 2021). Would the young persons of 2051 find that those pledges were indeed redeemed or regrettably recanted due to a lack of political will, weak resolve and inadequate commitment of resources to enable concerted global action?

Everyone alive today would be held responsible for the state of the world in 2051. If we succeed in the vision set for sustainable development in 2015 and deliver on the commitments to checkmate climate change, the world would be a better and safer place for the young persons of 2051. If we fail to do so and allow the drift to disaster to continue, the young persons of 2051 may be living in a present that they cannot repair and await a future that they cannot retrieve try as they might. The damage does become irreversible at some point of time.

Those who are young today would be middle-aged or older by 2051. They would be the ones asked to explain if the world is then in a terrible state. The older adults of today would mostly have exited from the world or be living in retired isolation, escaping accountability for their actions or inaction. The young persons of the future would either applaud their parents (the youth of today) for the efforts they made and the success they achieved in saving the world or berate them for their failure to protect future generations. So, it is those who are young today who have to act with strong resolve and smart strategy to change the models of human development.

Such changes cannot come only by behaviour change at the individual level. The dynamics of social change must recognize the complexity of connections across human society, between humans and other living forms and between nature and all life on earth. Understanding how such connections shape human health will help to appreciate why the phrase 'our common future' is much more meaningful than a mere political slogan. The connections indicate the levels at which corrections are needed. I hope the young persons of 2051 will be proud of what the young persons of 2021 have achieved.

Acknowledgements

This is a book I had been hoping to write for several years now. However, frenetic pace of the professional life I had chosen for myself did not permit the time needed to put my thoughts in order and place my fingers on the keyboard of my iPhone (I find it most convenient to write on that handy device). It was during the period of 'stay home–stop travel' discipline imposed by the COVID-19 pandemic that my mind resurrected the idea. It was a pleasant coincidence that Siddhesh Inamdar of HarperCollins India sent an email just at that time, enquiring if I was interested in writing a book. I readily accepted the invitation, and I am grateful to Siddhesh for sparking this effort.

As I started writing the book, Swati Chopra took charge as my editor. A soft-skilled and gently steering guide, she smoothly navigated me through the various stages of the publication process. I am beholden to her for displaying the calm and comforting demeanour of an experienced obstetrician while dealing with an author who anxiously posed questions like an expectant mother.

My colleagues were very supportive as I moved towards the final assembly of the chapters. Aji Chellappan acted as the assiduous assembler and careful custodian of the evolving drafts and helped to format them. Dr Manu Raj Mathur helped me with the compilation of references. Gina Sharma catalogued and curated the two forewords and a cascade of comments from the many eminent people who have endorsed this book. The support that I have received from all these friends reinforces the theme of this book: humans are indeed dependent on each other's goodwill and thrive best as a harmonious collective.

I am grateful to Saurav Das, who offered me several attractive cover options for the book. The final selection of the cover was with the help of my family members. My wife Sunanda is a developmental paediatrician, who became a devoted community organizer of health and social services for children with disabilities from low-income families in north-east Delhi. My daughter Shravya, who trained in law and international affairs, moved to engage with environmental policy and sustainability initiatives in Africa. My son Shreyas, a qualified aerospace engineer, is now a journalist in Korea and reports on issues of human security. Their eclectic pursuits, connected by a unifying world view and common commitment to humanitarian principles, enriched my thinking and energized me to write this book.

This book has also made me realize how blessed I am by the abundance of affectionate friendship that many eminent persons have most generously gifted me. The two forewords and the many praises, penned by some of the most brilliant global thinkers and earnest young changemakers, endow the book with wisdom that I could not have provided on my own. My heartfelt thanks to each of them.

Notes

Preface

1. Paine, Thomas. 1791. *Rights of Man.*

Why This Book?

1. Details available at https://www.brainyquote.com/quotes/sebastian_thrun_694788
2. Varshalomidze, Tamila and Usaid Siddiqui. "Leaders issue doomsday warning to tackle climate crisis'. *Climate Crisis News.*
3. Biermann, Frank and Rakhyun E. Kim. 2020. 'The boundaries of the planetary boundary framework: a critical appraisal of approaches to define a "safe operating space" for humanity'. *Annual Review of Environment and Resources*, 45: 497–521.
4. Wang-Erlandsson, Lan, *et al.* 2022. 'A planetary boundary for green water'. *Nature Reviews Earth & Environment*, 3: 380–392.
5. Details available at https://www.ncbi.nlm.nih.gov/books/NBK552471/
6. Schell, Jonathan. 1982. *The Fate of the Earth.* London: PICADOR.

Is It All in the Genes?

1. Details available at https://www.brainyquote.com/quotes/dan_buettner_551060
2. Collins, Francis S. 2003. 'Interview with Francis Collins'. Interview by Joseph McInerney, *The Natural Selection*, February, https://www.genome.gov/Pages/News/Documents/CollinsInterview.pdf
3. Ibid
4. Chaudhary, Rahul, Jalaj Garg, Neeraj Shah, and Andrew Sumner. 2017. 'PCSK9 inhibitors: a new era of lipid lowering rherapy', *World Journal of Cardiology* 9(2): 76–91.
5. Josefson, Deborah. 2001. 'Alzheimer's disease rarer among Nigerians than among African Americans'. *British Medical Journal* 322(7286): 574.
6. Details available at https://www.cdc.gov/cancer/breast/basic_info/risk_factors.htm#:~:text=Risk%20Factors%20You%20Cannot%20Change&text=Most%20breast%20cancers%20are%20diagnosed,Reproductive%20history.

Environment Fine-tunes Our Biology

1. Details available at https://www.forbes.com/quotes/9570/
2. Skirry, Justin. 2022. 'René Descartes: mind-body distinction', *Internet Encyclopedia of Philosophy*, https://iep.utm.edu/rene-descartes-mind-body-distinction-dualism/
3. Holmes, F. L. 1986. 'Claude Bernard: The milieu intérieur and regulatory physiology'. *History and Philosophy of the Life Sciences* 8(1): 3–25.
4. Davies, Kelvin J.A. 2016. 'Adaptive homeostasis'. *Molecular Aspects of Medicine* 49: 1–7.

5. Sterling, Peter and Joseph Eyer. 1988. 'Allostasis: A new paradigm to explain arousal pathology', in *Handbook of Life Stress, Cognition and Health*, pp. 629–39. New York: Wiley.

6. Chowdhury, Mohammad Asaduzzaman, Nayem Hossain, Mohammod Abul Kashem, Md Abdus Shahid, and Ashraful Alam. 2020. 'Immune response in COVID-19: A review'. *Journal of Infection and Public Health* 13(11): 1619–29.

7. Barrett, Lisa Feldman. 2020. *Seven and a Half Lessons About the Brain*. Boston: Mariner Books.

'I, Me, Myself'? Not Really!

1. Pasteur, Louis and Joseph Lister. 1996. *Germ Theory and Its Applications to Medicine and on the Antiseptic Principle of the Practice of Surgery*. New York: Prometheus Books.

2. Details available at https://www.rockefeller.edu/our-scientists/joshua-lederberg/2502-nobel-prize/#:~:text=Joshua%20Lederberg%2C%20Rockefeller%20University's%20fifth,to%20those%20of%20higher%20organisms.

3. Details available at http://www.Columbia.Edu/Itc/Hs/Pubhealth/P8475/Readings/Lederberg.Pdf

4. Collen, Alanna. 2015. *10% Human—How Your Body's Microbes Hold the Key to Health and Happiness*. Glasgow: William Collins

5. Lee, Elizabeth. 2019. 'We're only about 43% human, study shows', *VOA News*, 24 May, https://www.voanews.com/a/research-estimates-we-are-only-about-43-percent-human/4932876.html (accessed 30 November 2022).

6. Ursell, Luke K., Jessica L. Metcalf, Laura Wegener Parfrey, and Rob Knight.2012. 'Defining the human microbiome'. *Nutrition Reviews*, 70(Suppl 1): S38.

7. Ibid

8. Wook Kang, Dae. *et al.* 2017. 'Microbiota transfer therapy alters gut ecosystem and improves gastrointestinal and autism symptoms: an open-label study'. *Microbiome* 5(1): 1–16.

9. Wampach, Linda, *et al.* 2018. 'Birth mode is associated with earliest strain-conferred gut microbiome functions and immunostimulatory potential'. *Nature Communications* 9(1): 1–14.

10. Mueller, Noel T., Maria Gloria Dominguez-Bello, Lawrence J. Appel, and Suchitra K. Hourigan. 2020. '"Vaginal Seeding" after a caesarean section Provides Benefits to Newborn Children: FOR: Does Exposing Caesarean-Delivered Newborns to the Vaginal Microbiome Affect Their Chronic Disease Risk? The Critical Need for Trials of "Vaginal Seeding" during Caesarean Section'. *BJOG : An International Journal of Obstetrics and Gynaecology* 127(2): 301.

11. Saturio, Silvia, *et al.* 2021. 'Role of bifidobacteria on infant health'. *Microorganisms* 9(12): 2415.

12. Roxana, Tabakman. 2022. 'What role does the uterine microbiome play in fertility?', *Medscape*. 4 October, https://www.Medscape.Com/Viewarticle/981850 (accessed on 30 November 2022).

13. Moreno, I., *et al.* 2022. 'Endometrial microbiota composition is associated with reproductive outcome in infertile patients'. *Microbiome* 10(1): 1.

14. Details available at https://immunology.uchicago.edu/program/faculty/cathryn-r-nagler

15. Chen, Robert Y., *et al.* 2021. 'A microbiota-directed food intervention for undernourished children', *New England Journal of Medicine* 384(16): 1517–28.

16. Jeffery, Penny L., Michael A. McGuckin, and Sara K. Linden. 2011. 'Endocrine impact of Helicobacter Pylori: Focus on Ghrelin and Ghrelin o-Acyltransferase'. *World Journal of Gastroenterology* 17(10): 1249.

17. Cenit, Carmen, María, Yolanda Sanz, and Pilar Codoñer-Franch. 2017. 'Influence of gut microbiota on neuropsychiatric disorders'. *World Journal of Gastroenterology* 23(30): 5486.

18. Wu, Shaochang, Xia Liu, Ruilai Jiang, Xiumei Yan, and Zongxin Ling. 2021. 'Roles and mechanisms of gut microbiota in patients With Alzheimer's disease'. *Frontiers in Aging Neuroscience* 13: 650047.

19. Oh, Donghun and Keun Ah Cheon. 2020. 'Alteration of gut microbiota in autism spectrum disorder: an overview'. *Journal of the Korean Academy of Child and Adolescent Psychiatry* 31(3): 131.

20. Li, Nannan, Qi Wang, Yan Wang, Anji Sun, Yiwei Lin, Ye Jin, and Xiaobai Li. 2019. 'Fecal microbiota transplantation from chronic unpredictable mild stress mice donors affects anxiety-like and depression-like behavior in recipient mice via the gut microbiota-inflammation-brain axis'. *Stress* 22(5): 592–602.

21. Carlson, Alexander L. *et al*. 2018. 'Infant gut microbiome associated with cognitive development', *Biological Psychiatry* 83(2): 148–59.

22. Gao, Wei. *et al*. 2019. 'Gut microbiome and brain functional connectivity in infants-a preliminary study focusing on the Amygdala'. *Psychopharmacology* 236(5): 1641–51.

23. Bernard-Raichon, Lucie, *et al*. 2022. 'Gut microbiome dysbiosis in antibiotic-treated COVID-19 patients is associated with microbial translocation and bacteremia'. *Nature Communications* 13(1): 1–13.

24. Brooks, Megan. 2022. 'Unappreciated ties between COVID and gut dysbiosis,' *Medscape Medical News*, 1 November, https://www.medscape.com/viewarticle/983389 (accessed 30 November 2022).

25. Scimex, 'Centenarians have unique gut bugs that keep them going' *Scimex*, 2021, https://www.scimex.org/newsfeed/centenarians-have-unique-gut-bugs-that-keep-them-going#:~:text=They%20found%20that%2C%20compared%20with,acids%20through%20novel%20biosynthetic%20pathways.

Gene Expression Is Epigenetically Modulated Throughout Life

1. Details available at https://www.brainyquote.com/quotes/bruce_lipton_694107

2. Moore, Lisa D., Thuc Le, and Guoping Fan. 2013. 'DNA methylation and its basic function'. *Neuropsychopharmacology*, 23–38.

3. Albini, Sonia, Vlada Zakharova, and Slimane Ait-Si-Ali. 2019. 'Histone modifications'. *Epigenetics and Regeneration*, 47–72. allowing the concomitant neoexpression of specific genetic programs and silencing of others. Posttranslational modifications (PTMs)

4. Low, Felicia M., Peter D. Gluckman, and Mark A. Hanson. 2012. 'Developmental plasticity, epigenetics and human health'. *Evolutionary Biology*, 39(4): 650–65.

5. Geraghty, Aisling A., et al. 2015. 'Nutrition during pregnancy impacts offspring's epigenetic status—evidence from human and animal studies', *Nutrition and Metabolic Insights*, 8.Suppl 1: 41.

6. Ho, Shuk Mei, et al. 'Environmental epigenetics and its implication on disease risk and health'. *ILAR Journal*, 53(3–4): 289.

7. Williams, Louisa L. 2017. 'The five obstacles to cure: How to address the most common health challenges to optimal health'. *Wise Traditions in Food, Farming and the Healing Arts*, 18(2).

The Story of Stress

1. Details available at https://www.brainyquote.com/quotes/christopher_shays_217038

2. Tan, Siang Yong and A. Yip. 2018. 'Hans Selye (1907–1982): Founder of the Stress Theory', *Singapore Medical Journal*, 59(4): 170.

3. Details available at https://researchmatters.in/sciqs/chronic-stress-and-its-effects

4. Ozbay, Fatih, et al. 2007. 'Social support and resilience to stress: from neurobiology to clinical practice', *Psychiatry (Edgmont)*, 4(5).

5. Yaribeygi, Habib, et al. 2017. 'The impact of stress on body function: a review'. *EXCLI Journal*, 16.

6. Kolanowski, Wojciech, Katarzyna Ługowska, and Joanna Trafialek. 2022. 'Increased physical activity at school benefits arterial blood pressure in children—a prospective follow-up cohort study'. *International Journal of Environmental Research and Public Health*, 19(8).

7. NBCnews.com. 2018. 'The Science behind Being "Hangry"'. NBCnews.com

8. Details available at https://www.goodreads.com/author/quotes/119650.John_Hunter#:~:text=There%20are%20no%20actions%20without,both%20positive%20and%20negative%20effects.%E2%80%9D&text=%E2%80%9CThe%20ability%20to%20overcome%20failure,and%20move%20on%E2%80%94is%20crucial

Migration Mash-up: Gene-Environmental Interactions

1. Business Standard. 2013. 'Migrants Not "Pawns on Chessboard of Humanity", Pope Says'. *Business Standard.*

2. Dao, Thu Hien, et al. 2021. 'Global migration in the twentieth and twenty-first centuries: the unstoppable force of demography', *Review of World Economics*, 157(2): 417–49.

3. United Nations Department of Economic and Social Affairs, *Inequality in a Rapidly Changing World, World Social Report 2020*, Geneva: United Nations Department of Economic and Social Affairs.

4. Neel, James V. 2008. 'Thrifty Gene Hypothesis', in *Encyclopedia of Molecular Pharmacology*, pp. 1199–1199.

5. Speakman, J. R. 2008. 'Thrifty Genes for Obesity, an Attractive but Flawed Idea, and an Alternative Perspective: The "Drifty Gene" Hypothesis'. *International Journal of Obesity* 32(11): 1611–17.

6. Hales, C. Nicholas and David J.P. Barker. 2001. 'The thrifty phenotype hypothesis'. *British Medical Bulletin*, 60: 5–20.

7. Agyeman, C. and B J van Den Born. 2002. 'Cardiovascular health and disease in migrant populations: a call to action'. *Nat Rev Cardiol* 19(1-2).

8. Rosenthal, T., R.M. Touyz, and S. Oparil. 2022. 'Migrating populations and health: risk factors for cardiovascular disease and metabolic syndrome'. *Curr Hypertens Rep* 24: 325–340.

9. Poulter, N. *et al.* 1984. 'Blood pressure and its correlates in an african tribe in urban and rural environments', *Journal of Epidemiology and Community Health*, 38(3): 181–86.

10. Cheng, Ching Yu, *et al.* 2012. 'African ancestry and its correlation to Type 2 diabetes in African Americans: a genetic admixture analysis in three U.S. population cohorts'. *PLOS ONE*, 7(3): e32840.

11. Kagan, A., M.G. Marmot, and H. Kato. 1980. 'The Ni-Hon-San study of cardiovascular disease epidemiology'. In H. Kesteloot and J.V. Joossens (eds), *Epidemiology of Arterial Blood Pressure. Developments in Cardiovascular Medicine*, vol 8. Dordrecht: Springer.

12. McKeigue, P. M., G. J. Miller, and M. G. Marmot. 1989. 'Coronary heart disease in South Asians overseas: A review'. *Journal of Clinical Epidemiology*, 42(7): 597–609.

13. Gupta, Rajeev, *et al.* 2017. 'Recent trends in epidemiology of Dyslipidemias in India'. *Indian Heart Journal*, 69(3): 382–92.

14. Shah, Ebrahim, *et al.* 2010. 'The effect of rural-to-urban migration on obesity and diabetes in India: a cross-sectional study'. *PLoS Medicine*, 7(4).

15. Patel, J. V. , *et al.* 'Impact of migration on coronary heart disease risk factors: Comparison of Gujaratis in Britain and their contemporaries in villages of origin in India'. *Atherosclerosis*, 185(2): 297–306.

Selective Nutrients to Composite Diets

1. Details available at https://nutritionstudies.org/dr-t-colin-campbells-8th-principle-of-food-and-health/#:~:text=Good%20 nutrition%20creates%20health%20in,becomes%20part%20 of%20our%20body

2. Details available at https://www.nccih.nih.gov/health/ antioxidants-in-depth

3. Slavin, Joanne L. and Beate Lloyd. 2012. 'Health benefits of fruits and vegetables'. *Advances in Nutrition*, 3(4): 506.

4. Innes, Jacqueline K. and Philip C. Calder. 2018. 'The differential effects of Eicosapentaenoic Acid and Docosahexaenoic Acid on cardiometabolic risk factors: a systematic review'. *International Journal of Molecular Sciences*, 19(2).

5. Willcox, Donald Craig, Giovanni Scapagnini, and Bradley J. Willcox. 2014. 'Healthy aging diets other than the Mediterranean: a focus on the Okinawan diet', *Mechanisms of Ageing and Development*, 136–137: 148.

6. Mazzocchi, Alessandra, *et al.* 2019. 'The Secrets of the Mediterranean Diet. Does [Only] Olive Oil Matter?'. *Nutrients*, 11(12).

7. Joshipura, K. J. 2001. 'The effect of fruit and vegetable intake on risk for coronary heart disease', *Annals of Internal Medicine*, 134(12).

The Many Faces of Malnutrition

1. Details available at https://www.who.int/news-room/fact-sheets/ detail/malnutrition#:~:text=Poverty%20amplifies%20the%20 risk%20of,of%20poverty%20and%20ill%2Dhealth

2. Details available at https://www.who.int/news/item/19-11-2015- stunting-in-a-nutshell

3. Details available at https://www.who.int/data/gho/indicator- metadata-registry/imr-details/302#:~:text=Child%20wasting%20 refers%20to%20a,death%2C%20but%20treatment%20is%20 possible

4. Details available at https://www.sciencedirect.com/topics/ agricultural-and-biological-sciences/underweight

5. Greco, Emanuela A. *et al.* 2019. 'Epigenetic modifications induced by nutrients in early life phases: gender differences in metabolic alteration in adulthood'. *Frontiers in Genetics*, 10.

6. Kaveeshwar, Seema Abhijeet and Jon Cornwall. 2014. 'The current state of diabetes mellitus in India'. *The Australasian Medical Journal*, 7(1): 45.

7. Yoo, Eun Gyong. 2016. 'Waist-to-height ratio as a screening tool for obesity and cardiometabolic risk'. *Korean Journal of Pediatrics*, 425–31.

8. Details available at https://www.ifpri.org/sites/default/files/ ghi/2014/feature_1818.html#:~:text=The%20nature%20of%20 the%20malnutrition,and%20diet%2Drelated%20chronic%20 diseases

Agriculture, Food Systems and Health

1. Details available at https://www.fao.org/brussels/unfss-news/ detail/es/c/1402906/

2. Details available at https://www.glopan.org/sites/default/files/ pictures/GloPan%20Climate%20Brief%20Final.pdf

3. Details available at https://www.fao.org/forest-resources-assessment/remote-sensing/fra-2020-remote-sensing-survey/en/
4. Details available at https://ourworldindata.org/land-use-diets

Water Security and Sanitation Services

1. Details available at https://www.lshtm.ac.uk/aboutus/introducing/history/frieze/sir-edwin-chadwick
2. Tulchinsky, Theodore H. 2018. 'John Snow, cholera, the broad street pump; waterborne diseases then and now'. *Case Studies in Public Health*, 77.
3. Details available at https://www.who.int/news/item/18-06-2019-1-in-3-people-globally-do-not-have-access-to-safe-drinking-water-unicef-who
4. Details available at https://www.unicef.org/stories/7-fast-facts-about-toilets
5. Prüss, Annette, *et al.* 2002. 'Estimating the burden of disease from water, sanitation, and hygiene at a global level'. *Environmental Health Perspectives*, 110(5): 537.
6. Details available at https://www.keranews.org/2013-11-26/born-wet-human-babies-are-75-percent-water-then-comes-the-drying
7. Details available at https://www.un.org/sustainabledevelopment/water-and-sanitation/

Economic Development and Health: Growth and Equity

1. Details available at https://www.brainyquote.com/quotes/plutarch_109440
2. 'Preston, S.H. 1975. 'The Changing Relation between Mortality and Level of Economic Development'. *Popul. Stud. (Camb.)*, 29: 231–48.

3. Wilkinson, K. and Pickett, R. 2011. *The Spirit Level.* New York: Bloomsbury Publishing.

4. WHO Commission on Macroeconomics and Health & World Health Organization. 2001. Macroeconomics and health: investing in health for economic development: executive summary/report of the Commission on Macroeconomics and Health. World Health Organization.

5. Details available at https://onehealthtrust.org/projects/the-lancet-commission-on-investing-in-health/

6. Details available at https://annualreport.undp.org/2019/#:~:text=2019%20marked%20the%2010th,%2C%20and%2050%25%20by%202030

7. Details available at https://www.oxfam.org/en/research/time-care

8. Details available at https://www.oxfam.org/en/research/inequality-kills

9. UNDP

10. Details available at https://www.oxfam.org/en/research/time-care

11. Lancet Commission report on Investing in Health: Convergence by 2035, https://www.thelancet.com/commissions/global-health-2035)

Education and Health: A Close Relationship

1. Details available at https://quotefancy.com/quote/1601250/Joycelyn-Elders-I-feel-that-we-can-t-educate-children-who-are-not-healthy-and-we-can-t

2. UNESCO. 2018. *Education for Health and Well-Being.* Geneva: UNESCO.

3. Details available at https://uis.unesco.org/sites/default/files/documents/education-2030-incheon-framework-for-action-implementation-of-sdg4-2016-en_2.pdf

4. Details available at https://www.gaia.com/article/hunza-people-longevity-health-secrets

5. Details available at <https://hriday.org.in/about-us/.> 2022

Discrimination Creates Health Inequality

1. Details available at https://pnhp.org/news/getting-martin-luther-kings-words-right/

2. Maas, A. H.E.M. and Y. E.A. Appelman. 2010. 'Gender differences in coronary heart disease'. *Netherlands Heart Journal*, 18(12): 598.

3. Goli, Srinivas, Anu Rammohan, and Deepti Singh. 2015. 'The effect of early marriages and early childbearing on women's nutritional status in India', *Maternal and Child Health Journal*, 19(8): 1864–80.

4. Martin, Sandra L., *et al.* 1999. 'Domestic violence and sexually transmitted diseases: the experience of prenatal care patients'. *Public Health Reports*, 114(3): 262.

5. Quinn, Ashlinn K., *et al.* 2018. 'An analysis of efforts to scale up clean household energy for cooking around the world', *Energy for Sustainable Development*, 46: 1–10.

6. Manisalidis, Loannis, *et al.* 2020. 'Environmental and health impacts of air pollution: a review'. *Frontiers in Public Health*, 8: 14.

7. Parfitt, Barbara. 2015. 'Gender and health', in *The Routledge Handbook of Gender and Development*, pp. 250–60. London: Routledge.

8. Liu, Katherine A. and Natalie A. Dipietro Mager. 2016. 'Women's involvement in clinical trials: Historical perspective and future implications'. *Pharmacy Practice*, 14(1).

9. Warren, Penny. 2018. 'Julian Tudor Hart: visionary general practitioner who introduced the concept of the "inverse care law"', *BMJ*, 362.

10. WHO. 2017. 'World Bank and WHO: Half the world lacks access to essential health services, 100 million still pushed into extreme poverty because of health expenses', pp. 2017–20. WHO.

11. Details available at https://esv.literalword.com/

12. The New York Times. 2020. 'Dr. Susan Moore dies of Covid-19 after complaining of racism at Indiana hospital'. *The New York Times.*

13. Details available at https://www.nytimes.com/2020/12/23/us/susan-moore-black-doctor-indiana.html

14. The Hindu. 2021 'Migrant boat crossing from France to England capsizes; at Least 31 Dead'. *The Hindu.*

15. Roache, Madeline. 2022. 'How the Belarus-Poland dispute became a geopolitical crisis'. *Time.*

16. United Nations. 2007. *The Health Effects Of Global Warming: Developing Countries Are The Most Vulnerable.* Geneva: United Nations.

The Commercial Determinants of Health

1. Details available at https://www.goodreads.com/quotes/604382-people-are-fed-by-the-food-industry-which-pays-no#:~:text=%E2%80%9CPeople%20are%20fed%20by%20the%20food%20industry%2C%20which%20pays%20no,pays%20no%20attention%20to%20food.%E2%80%9D

2. Kickbusch, Ilona, Luke Allen, and Christian Franz. 2016. 'The commercial determinants of health'. *The Lancet Global Health*, 4(12): e895–96.

3. Details available at https://www.who.int/news-room/fact-sheets/detail/tobacco

4. Details available at https://fctc.org/what-is-the-fctc/

5. Details available at https://fctc.who.int/who-fctc/overview

6. Details available at https://www.who.int/news-room/fact-sheets/detail/alcohol

7. Gibney, Michael J. 2019. 'Ultra-processed foods: Definitions and policy issues'. *Current Developments in Nutrition*, 3(2).

8. Poti, Jennifer M., Meghan M. Slining, and Barry M. Popkin. 2014. 'Where are kids getting their empty calories? stores, schools, and fast food restaurants each play an important role in empty calorie intake among US children in 2009-2010'. *Journal of the Academy of Nutrition and Dietetics*, 114(6): 908.

9. Details available at https://www.cdc.gov/tobacco/data_statistics/ fact_sheets/tobacco_industry/hookahs/index.htm

10. Lin, S., *et al.* 2017.'Trends in diabetes and obesity in Samoa over 35 Years, 1978–2013'. *Diabetic Medicine*, 34(5): 654.

Universal Health Coverage

1. Details available at https://www.ncbi.nlm.nih.gov/pmc/articles/ PMC4541093/

2. Details available at https://www.ilo.org/global/publications/ world-of-work-magazine/articles/ilo-in-history/WCMS_120043/ lang--en/index.htm

3. Brown, Theodore M. and Elizabeth Fee, 'Rudolf Carl Virchow: Medical Scientist, Social Reformer, Role Model', *American Journal of Public Health*, 96(12).

4. Details available at https://www.parliament.uk/about/living-heritage/transformingsociety/livinglearning/coll-9-health1/coll-9-health/

5. Details available at https://www.who.int/publications/i/ item/9789241564021

6. Details available at https://www.who.int/data/gho/data/themes/ topics/indicator-groups/indicator-group-details/GHO/sdg-target-3.8-achieve-universal-health-coverage-(uhc)-including-financial-risk-protection

7. Jansen, P., L. Bijlmakers, N. Tromp, A. E. Yamin, and O. F. Norheim. 2017. 'Progressive realisation of universal health

coverage: what are the required processes and evidence?'. *BMJ Glob Health* 2(3): E000342.

8. Details available at https://blogs.worldbank.org/developmenttalk/what-lessons-social-protection-universal-health-coverage

9. Details available at http://www.uhc-india.org/reports/hleg_report.pdf

10. Details available at https://www.sciencedirect.com/topics/social-sciences/fee-for-service

11. Details available at https://www.sciencedirect.com/topics/social-sciences/capitation-fee

12. Details available at https://Sdg-Action.org/Covid-19-Strengthens-the-Case-for-Universal-Health-Coverage/

Our Healthcare Needs Other People Too

1. Details available at https://philosiblog.com/2013/03/13/to-know-even-one-life-has-breathed-easier-because-you-have-lived-this-is-to-have-succeeded/

2. Abraham Flexner and Herman Gates Weiskotten, 'The Flexner Report.' 1910.

3. Details available at https://www.who.int/news/item/02-06-2022-global-strategy-on-human-resources-for-health--workforce-2030

4. World Health Organization. 2020. 'Health Workforce: Medical Doctors', *Global Health Observatory (GHO) Data Repository*.

5. World Health Organization. Regional Office for South-East Asia. 2019. The Decade for Health Workforce Strengthening in the SEA Region 2015–2024: mid-term review of progress, 2020. World Health Organization. Regional Office for South-East Asia.

6. Karan, Anup, et al., 'Size, composition and distribution of health workforce in India: why, and where to invest?'. *Human Resources for Health*, 19(1).

7. Rao, Krishna D., Renu Shahrawat, and Aarushi Bhatnagar. 2016. 'Composition and distribution of the health workforce in India: estimates based on data from the National Sample Survey'. *WHO South-East Asia Journal of Public Health*, 5(2): 133–40.

Health Promotion Needs Social Policies

1. Details available at https://www.azquotes.com/quote/989589
2. Fallon, Cara Kiernan and Jason Karlawish. 2019. 'Is the WHO definition of health aging well? Frameworks for "health" after three score and ten'. *American Journal of Public Health*, 109(8).
3. Details available at https://www.who.int/teams/health-promotion/ enhanced-well-being/first-global-conference#:~:text=The%20 first%20International%20Conference%20on,health%20 movement%20around%20the%20world
4. Lalonde, M. 1974. *A New Perspective on the Health of Canadians*. Ottawa, ON: Minister of Supply and Services Canada.
5. Waldinger, Robert. 2017. 'Harvard study of adult development'. *Livestrong*, pp. 1–2.

On the Wings of Science and Technology

1. Details available at https://todayinsci.com/M/Mayo_William/ MayoWilliam-GloryQuote500px.htm
2. Details available at https://ourworldindata.org/
3. McNeil Jr., Donald G. 2001. 'Indian company offers to supply AIDS drugs at low cost in Africa', *New York Times*.
4. Details available at https://www.wto.org/english/tratop_e/dda_e/ dda_e.htm
5. Details available at https://unctad.org/system/files/official-document/diaeia2013d2_en.pdf
6. Details available at https://www.economist.com/ leaders/2015/08/08/time-to-fix-patents?gclid=Cjw

KCAiAkfucBhBBEiwAFjbkr3dUg7Zgh3N57Dc8J-
3FodL4fSz0Z0F6nLWYbldTg1HSth5HR-9MlhoCujQQAvD_
BwE&gclsrc=aw.ds

7. Vecchio, Ignazio, *et al.* 2018. 'The discovery of insulin: an important milestone in the history of medicine'. *Frontiers in Endocrinology*, 613.

8. Details available at https://www.vox.com/2019/4/3/18293950/why-is-insulin-so-expensive

9. Liu, Yongsheng, Baoyin Li, and Qinglian Wang. 2009. 'Science and Politics', *EMBO Reports* (European Molecular Biology Organization), 938–39.

Progress Should Not Impose Pollution Penalty on Health

1. Details available at http://edition.cnn.com/TRANSCRIPTS/0010/27/se.07.html

2. Details available at https://www.Britannica.Com/Topic/Air-Waters-and-Places

3. Details available at https://www.epa.gov/pm-pollution/particulate-matter-pm-basics

4. Kwon, Hyouk Soo, Min Hyung Ryu, and Christopher Carlsten. 2020. 'Ultrafine particles: unique physicochemical properties relevant to health and disease', *Experimental and Molecular Medicine*, 318–28.

5. World Health Organization. 2021. 'New WHO Global Air Quality Guidelines Aim to Save Millions of Lives from Air Pollution', *Air Pollution*, 1–300.

6. Calderón-Garcidueñas Lilian, *et al.* 2020. 'Alzheimer disease starts in childhood in polluted metropolitan Mexico City. a major health crisis in progress', *Environmental Research* 183:109137.

7. Details available at https://www.who.int/publications/i/item/9789240034228

8. Tulchinsky. Case Studies in Public Health. 2018 : 77–99. Published online 2018 Mar 30. doi: 10.1016/B978-0-12-804571-8.00017-2. PMCID: PMC7150208. John Snow, Cholera, the Broad Street Pump; Waterborne Diseases Then and Now Theodore H. Tulchinsky, MD MPH. https://www.ncbi.nlm.nih.gov/pmc/articles/PMC7150208/

9. Laville, Sandra. 2021. 'Southern water fined record £90m for deliberately pouring sewage into sea'. *The Guardian*.

10. Taneja, Neelam and Megha Sharma.2019. 'Antimicrobial resistance in the environment: The Indian scenario'. *Indian Journal of Medical Research*, 119–28.

11. Hachiya, Noriyuki. 2006. 'The history and the present of Minamata disease-entering the second half a century-investigation of causative agent and spread of the pollution occurrence of Minamata disease', *JMAJ*, 49(3).

12. Details available at https://www.unep.org/resources/report/minamata-convention-mercury

13. Larsen, Neil. 2021. 'Thomas Midgley, The Most Harmful Inventor in History', *OpenMind BBVA*.

Do Humans Trigger Zoonotic Pandemics?

1. Quammen D. 2012. *Spillover: Animal Infections and the Next Human Pandemic.* New York: W.W. Norton & Company, Inc

2. Details available at https://pubmed.ncbi.nlm.nih.gov/20945572/

3. Details available at https://www.emro.who.int/fr/about-who/rc61/zoonotic-diseases.html

4. Karen Steward. Antigenic Drift vs Antigenic Shift. Technology Networks: Immunology and Mircobiology. October 25, 2018.

https://www.technologynetworks.com/immunology/articles/
antigenic-drift-vs-antigenic-shift-311044

5. Details available at https://www.sciencedirect.com/topics/
immunology-and-microbiology/antigenic-shift

Loss of Biodiversity Harms Human Health

1. Details available at https://www.nationalgeographic.com/
environment/article/science-study-outlines-30-percent-
conservation-2030

2. Bar-On, Yinon M., Rob Phillips, and Ron Milo. 2018. 'The
biomass distribution on Earth'. *Proceedings of the National Academy
of Sciences of the United States of America*, 115(25): 6506–11.

3. 'Bioversity International. Research on Using Biodiversity to
Reduce Pests and Diseases' 2022. Pests and diseases https://
www.bioversityinternational.org/research-portfolio/agricultural-
ecosystems/pests-and-diseases/

4. Deutsch, Curtis A., *et al.* 2018. 'Increase in crop losses to insect
pests in a warming climate'. *Science*, 361(6405): 916–19.

5. El-Aziz, Tarek Mohamed Abd, Antonio Garcia Soares, and James
D. Stockand, 2019, 'Snake venoms in drug discovery: valuable
therapeutic tools for life saving'. *Toxins*, 11(10).

6. Gershlak, Joshua R., *et al.* 2017. 'Crossing kingdoms: using
decellularized plants as perfusable tissue engineering scaffolds'.
Biomaterials, 125: 13–22.

7. Details available at https://invention.si.edu/george-de-mestral-
velcro-inventor

8. Gershlak and others.Biomaterials Volume 125, May 2017,
Pages 13-22 https://www.sciencedirect.com/science/article/pii/
S0142961217300856

9. Details available at <https://www.youtube.com/watch?v=l
AzQWtkPzbI>

Health Hazards of a Planet in Peril

1. Stern, Nicholas. 2014. 'Summary of Conclusions', in *The Economics of Climate Change*. Cambridge: Cambridge University Press.
2. Pallavi Ghosh. 2020. 'Rise of the mosquitoes.' *Down to Earth*.
3. 'Bracing for superbugs: Strengthening environmental action in the One Health response to antimicrobial resistance'. UNEP, 7 Feb 2023.
4. 'Climate change is contributing to the rise of superbugs, new UN report says'. By Janelle Chavez, CNN Health News. 7 February 2023. https://edition.cnn.com/2023/02/07/health/superbugs-climate-change-scn
5. Details available at https://www.glopan.org/wp-content/uploads/2022/09/AgriculturalSubsidies.pdf

Vision of a Healthy Society

1. Venkatapuram, Sridhar. 2011. *Health Justice: An Argument from the Capabilities Approach*. New York: Wiley.
2. Details available at https://vigyanprasar.gov.in/pasteur-louis/
3. Details available at https://sdgs.un.org/goals

What Will the Young Persons of 2051 Say?

1. Details available at https://www.goodreads.com/author/quotes/141425.Paul_Val_ry

Index

About the Author

K. Srinath Reddy has lived in a multiverse of medicine, public health, sustainable development and public policy. Trained as a cardiologist and epidemiologist, he has been a passionate public health advocate at national and global levels. He was head of cardiology at the All India Institute of Medical Sciences, Delhi, before establishing the Public Health Foundation of India to create five Indian Institutes of Public Health. These are building broadband capacity in public health education, research, skill-building, policy development and programme implementation. After serving as the first Bernard Lown Visiting Professor of Global Cardiovascular Health at Harvard, he is presently an Adjunct Professor at Harvard, Emory, Pennsylvania and Sydney universities.

Reddy was President of the World Heart Federation and is co-chair of the Health Thematic Group of the UN Sustainable Solutions Network. Author of 570 scientific papers and the book *Make Health in India*, he is an International Member of the US National Academy of Medicine and has served on several technical committees of the WHO. He chaired the High Level Expert Group on Universal Health Coverage for India's Planning Commission and advises several Indian states on health policy.

Reddy has received the WHO Director General's Award and the Luther Terry Medal of the American Cancer Society for outstanding global leadership in tobacco control, besides the Queen Elizabeth Medal for Health Promotion and several honorary doctorates. The President of India conferred on him the prestigious civilian honour Padma Bhushan in 2005.

30 Years *of*

![HarperCollins logo] HarperCollins *Publishers* India

At HarperCollins, we believe in telling the best stories and finding the widest possible readership for our books in every format possible. We started publishing 30 years ago; a great deal has changed since then, but what has remained constant is the passion with which our authors write their books, the love with which readers receive them, and the sheer joy and excitement that we as publishers feel in being a part of the publishing process.

Over the years, we've had the pleasure of publishing some of the finest writing from the subcontinent and around the world, and some of the biggest bestsellers in India's publishing history. Our books and authors have won a phenomenal range of awards, and we ourselves have been named Publisher of the Year the greatest number of times. But nothing has meant more to us than the fact that millions of people have read the books we published, and somewhere, a book of ours might have made a difference.

As we step into our fourth decade, we go back to that one word – a word which has been a driving force for us all these years.

Read.